"Naked into the Wilderness"

PRIMITIVE
WILDERNESS LIVING
& SURVIVAL SKILLS

by John & Geri McPherson

Prairie Wolf

P.O. Box 96 • Randolph, KS 66554

THIS BOOK IS
DEDICATED TO
THE MEMORY OF

A Co.; 1/503rd Inf.
173rd Airborne Brigade (Sep)

KIA
5 FEB. 1967

WHO UNWITTINGLY GUIDED
ME ON THE PATH
TO WHAT I AM TODAY

CONTENTS

Contents (con't.)

INTRODUCTION

In the spring of 1986 I, John, first published a 48 page book on brain tanning. I had spent years searching for - mostly thru trial and error - a recipe for this project. I had found nothing in print that was to be of much help.

Several years earlier I had begun looking for some way to live more closely with nature. Even as a child I was aware that there had been a day at one point in the past that man had lived directly with the earth. Modern society had taken us far away from that.

I suppose that 1972 was the year that I began my search in earnest. I didn't know where I was heading ... I didn't know where to begin. I just knew that I wanted a more natural way of life ... at the time not even knowing just what that meant.

My search began with back to the basics ... a movement that seemed to have really begun nationwide in the '60's. I got a small parcel of land ... began work on my own house, had hogs, a calf, garden - *self-sufficiency at its best*.

I began to seriously dabble in the *primitive* in the mid-'70's. I attempted to brain tan a calf skin. I made (and broke) my first bow. The first friction fire appeared (bow drill - it took three of us half a day).

Then this was all placed on the back burner as the more important and pressing day to day survival of the present took over. It was after this first jump into the primitive that the homesteading spirit took hold. All time and efforts were put towards *modern* self-sufficiency.

At the beginning of the '80's my wife of the moment (my 2nd) began heading towards the more modern world ... I began to fall backwards, to *progress thru regression* as Geri, who I refer to (with a smile) as my *current* wife, says.

The term self-sufficiency began to take on a whole new meaning for me. Tho I did find myself much more self reliant than the vast majority of men of the modern world, I was still dependent on someone for something. Gasoline. Tools. Metal & steel. Utensils. Clothing. Seed. Fencing. Repair parts for machinery. Tires. Then list was long.

Yeah, I had read and heard of those who were more self reliant in the fact that they did away with some of the above ... using horses for tractors, rails for fencing, etc. But I still found that they all had some dependency on *someone* for *something*.

So where to begin? Back to rubbing sticks for fire. I mentally placed myself "NAKED IN THE WILDERNESS". What, I thought, just **what** was necessary for me to know if ever I was to place myself in the wilds with nothing. That put a whole new light on the phrase self-sufficiency.

This, I found, took more than just a little thinking. Food/shelter/ clothing - the first things to come to mind. Great. How to obtain food, make shelters and clothing? How about some tools? Fire? String (cordage)? Weapons or traps to get the food? ... and also skins to turn into material?

"Hey buddy", says I," this ain't gonna be so easy." And it wasn't.

Where does one begin to learn these skills, so long ago lost. With the Native American Indians of course.

So off to the library I goes in search of *primitive*. Everything I find on Indians I devour.

But, the Indians, it seems, had lost the ability to live with the land the same as the white eye. I found nothing but vague references to primitive skills such as cording/friction fire and tanning with brains.

The same when I turned to what skills books that I could find. It seems that the authors of these books had only read of these skills - or heard of them from others. If some of them did know, they didn't seem to be telling all. Some had compiled works of others not knowing just what they were compiling as they themselves didn't knowenough about the subjects to verify whether it worked or not. In such manner is the myth perpetuated. Some authors might have known their subjects but were unable to translate it to me. Whatever, one dead end after another.

Much time was spent in *doing*. I mean, what else was there to do. I had to try to separate fact from mythology, and believe me there was, and is, a lot of perpetuated myth out there in primitive skills land.

Sure, I did have some head start. I at least knew that it was wood that was rubbed together to make fire, not sea shells. But there is a lot more to it than that. *(Later learnings certainly were accelerated thru contact with other primitives - some more willing than others to share their knowledge.)*

I began to associate with the modern mountain man in 1985 when I first attended a rendezvous, a national one held in the Colorado Rockies. At this first contact with others trying to hold onto primitive skills, I discovered that there were only a handful of people in a camp of over 800 lodges who were wearing brain tan.

"Why?", asks I. "Too difficult", says they. "Not so", responds I. And so, the first book was born.

Thru these rendezvous I began to teach, first tanning, then friction fire making. Bow and arrow making followed. Books on these seemed to follow naturally.

In 1987 Geri and I made acquaintance. Two peas in a pod. We married shortly there-after.

What began as one book for one audience grew into a *series* for everyone - because everyone, it seems, has some interest in taking some control in their lives. Even something as insignificant as making their own shoe string. Something that they can point to with pride and say "I made that".

Ten books have been written. The last off the press just a coupla days back. Thousands of people have been buying these, Some interested in only one or two aspects ... others interested in the entire realm. To date we have in print over 110,000 books. 33,000 of our first, Brain Tan Buckskin, alone. People want this. They have been looking and they haven't been finding. Those who know and practice (or who are seriously trying to learn) primitive skills are aware of what is out there. Most is trash. It might make for interesting reading but it just don't work in a "how-to" situation. Line drawings are used for the most part because it takes a finished product to photograph and many aren't capable of this.

What we illustrate here are methods that do work. Take note that these are not the only methods that work. It's just the way that we do things. If you follow the instructions put forth here, you will be successful.

So what we have is a compilation of our ten books - here ten *chapters*. Why? ... *business*. Hate to admit it.

When we had one, two or even five books we could kinda afford to keep printing and reprinting ... and reprinting. Really, it just got to be quite an expensive hobby. Everyone said to raise the price - always kept at $3.00. Sure, folks would pay more but we just couldn't justify charging more for what actually costs us around 50 cents.

Of course not being business people we never took into account all the people in between you and us that have to make a living too ... and they do it better than us. So, after we printed the tenth (to be fair to those who have the rest of the series but don't want to buy the whole volume to fill it out) we finally felt that to afford to keep going we were compelled to combine them. This makes it easier on us both logistically and financially and also makes it somewhat less expensive for you, the reader.

In this compilation, we have simply printed the original books as they were, pulling unnecessary pages and changing a word or phrase here and there. We have elected to keep the original introductions to each book as an introduction to its appropriate chapter so as to show you how we were thinking at each stage and to measure our progress.

This book is for the person who wants to *learn* primitive skills, not read about them. It works.

We thank Romelle Van Sickle of Riley, KS for her untiring efforts in helping put together the first books of this series. Without her help and support this may never have come into being.

John & Geri McPherson
January 1993

Much personal assistance provided by **all** the folks at the printers;
AG Press
Box 1009
Manhattan, KS 66502
(913) 539-7558
contact: Terrie Clark

1

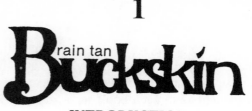

Brain tan Buckskin

INTRODUCTION

My first attempt at tanning with brain was in 1974. At that time I could locate very few sources pertaining to this subject. What I did come up with left a lot to be desired. My results were quite unsuccessful but enough small bits of the skin did work out to give me hope and show me what could be accomplished if done properly. (I had no idea at this time what real buckskin was even like. I had read only vague references to Indian tanned skins). All of what I could find on this subject was written by someone who had no "hands on" experience but was writing what had been observed or heard. That may not be a bad way to describe a procedure but is hardly the way to write a "how to".

With more and more interest shown in "back to basics" since then, and especially the blossoming interest in buckskinning, more has been written about some of the natural/primitive ways and skills. It is not as difficult now to find a "how to" book written on about any subject one may want to venture into. I sure haven't had the opportunity to read all that has been written on brain tanning. I probably don't even know the existance of half of it. From what I have read however, combined with my personal recent experiences of trying to learn more about it, I feel that I have done a lot better.

Most of what I have read recently, if read by someone not at all familiar with the procedure, (and to my way of thinking "how to" books and articles should be addressed to those who don't know "how to") leaves the reader with a lot of questions unanswered. If read with no other purpose than the joy of reading or to somewhat further one's knowledge...fine. But most don't work for the individual interested in taking a raw deer skin and turning it into a fine piece of material...especially if that individual hardly knows what a deer is.

This book was deliberately written to over-simplify because IT SIMPLY IS NOT AS DIFFICULT AS MOST ACCOUNTS TEND TO MAKE IT APPEAR! But do not belittle the amount of effort required when I demonstrate that it can be done in as little as 9 hours. . .that 9 hours is considering IDEAL WORKING CONDITIONS. There are many, many variables that can and do effect the quality of the finished product.

It is frustrating and time consuming to have to search out numerous sources to learn a new skill. I have tried to make this as complete and easy to follow as what I wanted and needed when I did my first skin. I have had it read by uninformed people, both male and female, and tried to incorporate their suggestions for clarity. I want this booklet to work. It was designed so that the interested and motivated person with no foreknowledge at all in skins could take this booklet, a raw deer skin, very minimal materials and end up with a finished buckskin. I'm satisfied that it will do that.

I would strongly suggest that one take this book and read it carefully. Study the photographs...re-read...learn what is happening to the skin...and why. Go over the various steps until you know what each is accomplishing. Some parts of this may seem complicated when you first read it, but if you study it closely you will find that I'm trying to make it easier and faster for you...such as the lacing into the frame. You can lace it any damn way that you want, and for one skin maybe you should. But I feel certain that when you find how simple and quickly that you can make buckskin, you'll not stop at one.

I speak throughout of the average 10 square foot deer skin, that's a large skin. Actually the deer we have in northcentral Kansas average larger than that. Smaller skins will require less time and effort. I have deliberately not gone into the making of anything but buckskin so as to keep it as simple as possible. You'll find nothing about working larger hides or furs. Basic principles are the same but there are certain differences for each.

As with anything worthwhile, it will take some effort and sweat...but not nearly what most have been led to believe. There is no secret...only simple rules.

Have at it!

April 1986

11

BRIEF, ALL IMPORTANT, SUMMARY

So pay attention. What I describe here may not actually be the scientific facts that some are searching for...but if you understand what is put forth here you will know what is happening to the skin...and why. This knowledge will not only help you to better approach the task at hand, but will also be invaluable in troubleshooting and correcting mistakes.

First you must understand the product which you are working with, the skin.

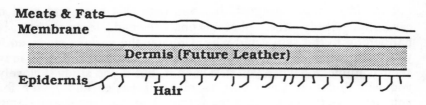

The future leather (the dermis) is actually millions of tiny threads. You MUST visualize this (note photo. pg. 43)..think of it as very compressed cotton. An inherent property of these threads is glue. Boil them down and you have hide glue. Oils, in our case from the brains, (10W motor oil might work...Ivory soap does..just not as well as brains) are penetrated COMPLETELY through the dermis to coat all of these threads. In the methods illustrated here, the brains (oils) are mixed with water...water is thinner than the oils and therefore penetrates easier and faster...BUT...the oils will not penetrate through the membranes, sandwiching either side of the skin. Water will. Oils won't. Therefore the necessity of removing these membranes. The inner membrane, which is a solid sheet, is easily removed, most times completely, while fleshing. Sandpaper will show where this has been missed. The outer membrane, the epidermis, is no harder nor more or less important to remove than the inner...BUT...it is the hardest for you to LEARN to remove. The epedermis is not a solid sheet..in fact it more compares to sandpaper, millions of tiny dots...the grain of leather. This is removed, in our method, by dry scraping. Removing the hair and the epidermis at the same time. Your scraper will remove hair and epidermis from an area about 1/4 inch at a lick...work an area about 1 inch wide...overlap your strokes...let your eyes penetrate into the skin...you will eventually see what you are removing. It DOES NOT look the same all over the skin. It may take 10 to 12 strokes before you have successfully removed the epidermis from your 1 inch wide strip. PAY ATTENTION.

Once the surfaces are prepared, the oils will be able to penetrate. We need to coat EVERY fiber with these oils...therefore the repeated applications...you cannot overbrain. But, once oiled, if left unattended, the skin will shrink and dry hard (the glue taking effect) ... but, if you are to MOVE THESE LUBRI- CATED FIBERS UPON THEMSELVES while the skin dries, the oils will allow the FIBERS TO STAY SEPARATED AND THEY WILL SWELL SOMEWHAT...the result...unbelievably soft flannel-like leather.

Now if this was to be wetted, the fibers would again shrink and dry hard (the glue) unless worked. BUT...if we penetrate the entire, loosely woven skin with smoke, the pitch will WATERPROOF THE FIBERS...the skin itself is not waterproofed. Water will run through it....but the fibers will be waterproofed..and the wetted skin will again dry soft since the water has not been allowed to get to the INDIVIDUAL FIBER and allow the glue to take effect.

Once you understand this, you are in control.

(I became aware of the glue action above mentioned thru Jim Rigg's book *"Blue Mountain Buckskin"*--the importance of always learning.)

Now, a note pertaining to finishing the skin out. I describe here-in finishing it out by pulling over a rope...or also by hand. Many, many others accomplish the same by a method described as "staking"...after braining, lacing the skin back onto the frame and working the fibers by applying force with a rounded stick.

I think of the skin, stretched on the frame after fleshing as being stretched 100%. When the skin has been cut from the frame and after braining, worked by hand, IT WILL SHRINK ABOUT 20%. When staked, the skin will stretch another 5 to 10%...to it's limits.

On the one hand, you end up with a larger skin. On the other, the skin, though 25-30% smaller, is also that much thicker..and spongier...and stretchier. To me it is alive yet.

One advantage to working the skin by hand...at any time it can be rolled up, placed in a plastic bag and frozen until what time you want to get back to it. Once you begin staking...you'll stake till you're done.

The only <u>tool</u> necessary to end up with buckskin

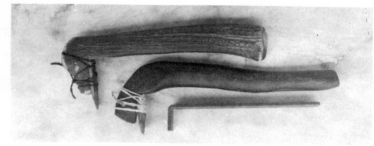

Top: Elk antler handle w/steel blade-.Middle: Wooden Osage Orange handle w/flint blade. Bottom: Steel Handle.

Left: Front view of file blade. Roundness prevents tearing into skin. Right: Side view-extreme angle is put on w/grinder at approx. 20-25°--working angle of approx. 45° is put on with whetstone (line).

A SIMPLE BREAKDOWN

	STEP	TOTAL HOURS
Day 1		
6:30 - 8 a.m.	Frame and flesh	1½
12 - 12:30 p.m.	Prepare flesh side	½
3 - 4:30 p.m.	Dehair	1½
4:30 - 5 p.m.	Prepare hair side	½
5 - 6:15 p.m.	Prepare and apply brains	1¼
6:15 - 6:45 p.m.	Stretch skin open and wrap in towels/refrigerate	½
Day 2		
8 - 11 a.m.	Finish stretching	3
	TOTAL HOURS	8¾

During the afternoon of the second day the skin could be smoked. This simplified schedule is figuring ideal weather for drying.

MATERIALS

Every "How To" book needs a list of materials. This is ours.

A big advantage of tanning (dressing) your skins with brains is the minimum of expenditure required for materials. Most, if not all, will be on hand in the average home.

Knife - a pocket or paring knife is all that is necessary. The only requirements are a thin sharp blade and a good point.

4 **2x4's** about 8 ft. long and **nails.** Cedar or pine poles lashed and/or nailed securely will work fine. It must be a good solid frame.

125-150 ft. of **1/8 in. nylon cord** in 25-30 ft. lengths -- or whatever else that you come up with. Nylon is easy to work with and long lasting.

Sandpaper - # 50 coarse grit works well for medium and larger skins. Use a finer grit for smaller, thinner skins.

Brains - I have heard tell of others using liver, pancreas and other oily organs. I have never used anything but brains. The brain from the critter was used "back then". Mine comes packaged neatly in one-pound plastic containers from the local supermarket. Get yours where you can.

Bucket - something in the 2 to 3 gallon size is convenient. Material doesn't matter.

A **wringer** from an old wringer washer. Certainly not very primitive or natural but sure does work well. (The stick is the natural way)

15-20 ft. of good tight **heavy rope**. The best that I have found is a lariat. Definitely something that won't unravel as you rub the skin back and forth across it, and at least ½" in diameter.

Scraper - The Indians used a section of elk antler with either a flint or, in later times, steel blade attached to work their skins and hides. I used one once and found it ideal. With no access to elk antlers in northeast Kansas I used the next best, Osage orange. Any hard wood will suffice, the heavier the better.

SCRAPER: Handle from osage orange...blade from file.

I used a dead piece about 2" in diameter and 18" long with a limb protruding at a 90° angle at one end. After debarking, scraping and sanding smooth, I sawed into the knot at a 90° angle a platform on which to tie the blade. The blade was made from a section of old file (any hard steel will work, a file is usually handy) about 3" long, rounded on one end and a 45° angle edge applied. This is tied to the handle and you're ready to go.

The first two skins I did were done with a well rounded, heavy skinning knife. And several were finished using a hog scraper, well rounded. I have even used an old hand-held flint scraper I found in an old campsite-once.

Not all skins need to be extra large No. 1. This small "Bambi" with large cut still made a nice 6 square foot skin.

SKINS

Acquiring deer skins is not really difficult. There are many sources from which you may obtain them if you look and ask around.

During deer season I can acquire 15-20 from friends and acquaintances who have no use for them. There are also a number of locker plants in the area from which I can obtain as many as I want by paying the going rate-sometimes for as little as $2.00, but normally closer to $5. Contact with local law and game enforcement officers also informs me of many road kills.

Wherever you get them, some words of caution. Most hunters who skin their own, and all butchers that I have run across, take great pride in how fast they can remove the skin from the deer. The quicker and the cleaner that the skin is removed does no favors for the tanner but only leaves numerous holes and scores (cuts into the skin not deep enough to be holes--yet).

When I skin a deer it takes me from 15 to 30 minutes to do the job, depending on whether it's done in the field or from the front-end loader of a tractor. When the skin is to be tanned I am not a fast skinner; I am careful. The knife is used sparingly and I leave all stubborn bits of meat and fat on the skin. They come off easily enough later with no appreciable loss of meat to the hunter. By being a bit more careful I don't end up with a skin full of holes, or worse yet, the many, many scores that can take a good number one skin and turn it into a piece of crap. Light scores on the thicker part of the skin, such as the neck, are usually acceptable, but the normal score on the average part of the skin will, nine times out of ten, tear out while you are working the skin in the final stretching process. BEWARE OF SCORES!

In order to collect as many good skins as possible, I will often offer to skin them out for the local hunters and they are usually pleased as punch to have me do this for them-especially when it's as cold as it can get around here in December. As an added bonus I'm almost always allowed to remove the loin sinew strips also.

From the butcher: Well, you pretty well have to take what you can get. Just prior to the season I always go around to the processors with whom I've made arrangements and ask them to please use the knife sparingly. This usually helps.

There are three common ways to keep the skins until you are ready to tan them. The oldest way is to just leave them exposed to the air until they are dry. This is also the most time consuming later as it must be soaked in fresh water for what seems like forever to make it as soft and pliable as when green.

Salting the skin for preservation is probably the most commonly used method. The flesh side is coated liberally with salt and the excess moisture allowed to drain off-it will keep this way for 6-8 months before needing to be resalted. Though it most assuredly works, I don't personally use this method as it requires a lot of time and water to wash out the salt, all of which must be removed. Salt draws moisture. Unsmoked brain tan dries stiff if moistened.

By far the easiest way to keep them is to freeze them. I do this as soon after collecting the skin as I can by rolling it, hair side out, tying it in a tight, neat bundle and placing it in an airtight plastic bag. I am now tanning skins that have been frozen this way for three years. I believe that they could be kept forever this way and still be as green and fresh when thawed as the day they were put up, but you need to keep air from the flesh side. By keeping the skin frozen I eliminate any need to wash or soak the skin before tanning, which saves considerable time, energy and water. Only the bloodiest of skins will I even wash. The skin will dry considerably faster and be ready to work sooner if the hair is not moistened.

FRAMING AND FLESHING

Now let's do something with that skin, wherever it came from.

If it was dried, then you would do best to find a source of running water, such as a stream, and weight it with rocks and leave for a coupla days or so. It will take a long time to get it back to the same state it was in when taken from the deer. You do need to check it every so often to insure that the fresh water is getting to the entire skin. If you don't have access to a creek or a stream, place it into a large container, such as a 25 gallon trash can and soak. The water must be changed regularly; after only a coupla hours the first few times, and probably at least every 10-12 hours from then on until it is workable. On warmer days be sure that the water doesn't heat enough to rot the skin. It needs to soak until as pliable and fresh as when removed from the deer.

A salted skin is more easily prepared. It needs only repeated washings to remove ALL of the salt.

Frozen skins need only to be thawed.

When ready, roll it out on a level surface and trim the perimeter to remove all rough edges, including the lower legs. The skin can, of course, be tanned with the legs on but it adds considerable work. Right now let's get you proficient at making buckskin. You can do any extras later after you get the basics mastered.

When the skin is trimmed, stretch it to it's natural shape and lay the 2x4's around it, nailing them together, two nails per corner. We want to build the frame about 8-10 inches larger on all sides of the skin as the skin stretches considerable while being fleshed. While nailing the frame together, fold the skin on itself to prevent it from drying. You will probably want to apply water to the flesh side at intervals to keep it fresh until you're finished fleshing.

Now to lace the skin to the frame--place it on the ground or work table flesh side up and punch holes around the entire perimeter of the skin with a thin bladed knife. The holes are to be ½ - 1" from the edge and approximately 1½" apart. The easiest way to make these holes is to place a board under the skin, push the point of the knife against the skin into the board with one hand and pull the skin up with the other. I say to use a thin blade because you don't want the holes too large.

To keep the natural shape of the skin square within the frame as you lace, I have found it convenient to tie each corner of the skin to the corresponding corner of the frame with a 12 - 15" cord. Also place the skin just a little off center to the right (as you face it from the bottom). After having done a few skins you will find no need to tie the corners in order to square it within the frame but it sure helps the beginner.

UPPER LEFT: Frame built around skins. RIGHT: Laced on three sides.
LOWER: Completely laced.

Picture the frame in an upright position with the neck at the top and the flesh side facing you. You will begin lacing at the neck at the upper left corner. From that corner, go through the hole at the corner of the neck, out under the 2x4 and in over it again to the skin. Now begin to take the cord through three holes at a time as if you were sewing--the cord, as it passes through the series of three holes, runs in and out in a straight line, not wrapped around the edge. Then take the cord out under the frame and in over it and then do three more holes. The cord always comes from the skin out under the frame and back over it to the skin. I normally go through three holes at a lick, sometimes two and very seldom four, but only as long as the holes are in a straight line. This is to save the inconvenience of having to relace if one of the holes rips out. As the edge of the skin turns at legs, corners, etc., bring your cord around the frame and begin your series of holes again. At the neck where the skin is the thickest I will go through only one hole if that's the way the count ends up at a corner.

Do not pull the cord too tightly but just "snug it up" for now. When you reach the end of one length of cord, tie it off and begin with another. I will normally leave two or three holes (one series) for the rope that I tied off to go through as I take up the slack. As you round the second corner and begin the bottom, you can begin to take up some of the slack...but not too tight now or you will lose your shape. (Never pull too tightly on the bottom as it will easily tear.) After you go around the third corner and into the home stretch, you can really begin to tighten things up, even going back to the bottom section and taking up the remainder of the slack there. By the time that you reach the neck, from whence you began, the skin will be fairly taunt and close to being centered on the frame.

If the skin seems to dry some while the lacing process is going on, simply splash water on it to keep it wet. For now you want the skin kept fresh and pliable.

Now stand the frame, neck up, against a tree, the side of a shed, etc. It is best to keep the skin in the shade at this stage to keep it from drying too fast as you flesh. It's a good idea to always keep the frame tied so that a sudden gust of wind doesn't send it flying. Now beginning at the neck, tighten the ropes all around the skin until it's as tight as a drum on the frame. You will have to re-tighten these as you flesh for the skin will stretch considerably.

Taking the scraper (I like it very sharp but you must be extremely careful not to cut into the skin itself), begin at the neck and remove every bit of the meat, fat and membrane that you possibly can. The knife will come in handy here at certain spots, such as around the legs and along the edges. With some skins,

23

this will be an easy job. With others, such as the old timer trophy buck, your work will be cut out for you. You may be tempted on some of these heavier skins to leave quite a bit on until the next step, but believe me, now is the time to remove it. It's damn near impossible to remove all of the membrane at this point, but get what you can. Definitely get all of the meat and fat off.

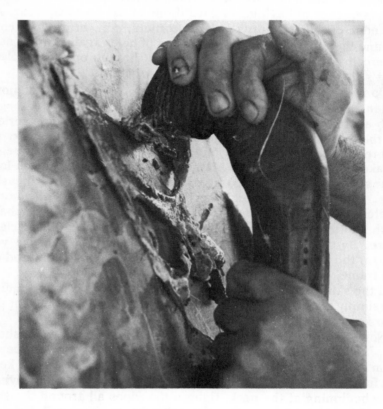

Flesh, fats and membrane easily removed with scraper.

Do not attempt to clean all the way to the edge or you will end up cutting the cords and/or ripping out the holes. The perimeter is cut off later and discarded.

Keep the skin tight within the frame. It fleshes much easier than a loose, sloppy one with a lot less chance of cutting into it with the scraper.

Neck and right side fleshed clean.
Note remaining layer of flesh on left
side. All must be removed.

Once the skin is as clean as you can get it, leave it and go on to something else for awhile. You can do nothing further with it until it is completely dry and with the high humidity here in northeast Kansas that can take from six to eight hours on a good day. Drier climates will, of course, make drying considerably faster.

SURFACE PREPARATION

When the stretched skin has dried COMPLETELY, both sides must now be prepared so that the brain will be allowed to penetrate completely into the thickest areas.

I have read and heard that the skin should not be allowed to dry in the sun, for various reasons, but I have many times left it in the full sun to help speed the drying process and have found that it makes no difference what-so-ever in the working of, or the final condition of, the finished product. It does cause some curling of the skin because of uneven drying but that hasn't yet interfered in my working of it. The hair side will naturally take longer to dry completely to the roots and epidermis and if anxious to proceed you might fluff the hair occasionally with a brush.

Leveling high spot of score with very sharp scraper.

Figuring that you're anxiously awaiting the skin to dry enough so as to continue the operation, we'll begin with the flesh side when IT IS GOOD AND DRY. This will be about midway to when the hair side is ready. Begin with the SHARP scraper and work LIGHTLY around the neck area down to the shoulders and all the way around the perimeter of the skin. These are the areas where you most likely left on some of the membrane, which must be completely removed for the brain to penetrate into the skin itself. (Water, a liquid, will penetrate this. Brain and its accompanying oils are thicker and will not penetrate through this membrane, nor through the epidermis on the other side). Carefully work the scraper around the rough high areas of any scores, in the direction that they lie, never across them, to even these areas off. Also carefully work the scraper around any holes.

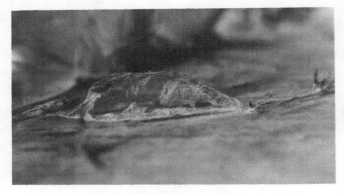

Membrane on flesh side.

Now take sandpaper and go over every inch of the surface to remove any small bits of membrane and to level the surface. This will also have the added benefit of "bringing up the nap" which will allow better absorbancy of the brain. Sand the neck area first and then do a strip around the entire perimeter a coupla inches wide. Divide the remainder into quarters and sand them one at a time until you are positive that every square inch has been covered. This method helps to insure that every last bit is clean and smooth. Missing even one small area can result in a rough, stiff spot. Start the sanding with long strokes, using a block, and finish off by using the sandpaper in your hand so that isolated, deliberate finger pressure can be applied where necessary. When finished most of the surface will be soft and fluffy. This side is ready for the application of the brain, but, of course, we will need to work the other side first. (A fur would now be ready but there are some different rules to follow with those which we won't delve into here. In this book we are sticking to the making of buckskin).

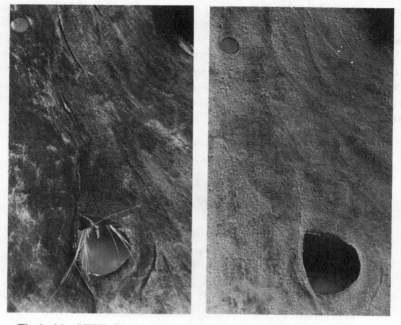

Flesh side. LEFT: Fleshed and dried. RIGHT: High areas scraped and sanded...ready for brain.

To prepare the hair side take the very sharp scraper and begin at the neck and "scrape" the hair off. With a heavy, sharp scraper this is not much of a chore. First clean a strip across the top of the skin (neck). Now with long, powerful downward strokes of the scraper the hair will readily come off. You will need to sharpen the blade several times during this process...you want it sharp. At the legs and at the flanks the hair lies in different directions and you will have to scrape in different directions to get it to come off easily. For most of the body of the skin good powerful, downward strokes is what will work best. Apply less pressure around the legs

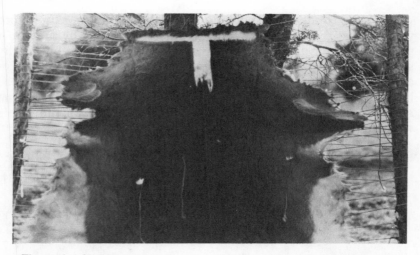

First strip of hair scraped across top. Note hanging cords marking holes.

and at the flanks. It is wise to leave the flanks till last and then scrape them with a freshly sharpened blade and apply as little pressure as needed. Should you happen to "pop" a hole then, it won't interfere with the scraping of the rest of the skin. It is tricky to remove the hair from around one of these holes that just seem to "pop" up.

Cut caused by use of too coarse of sandpaper.

29

It is wise to mark any existing holes already in the skin before you begin as the hair hides them completely. Do this by running a piece of rope or a small stick through each which can be readily seen as you are dehairing. It is easy to forget that they are there and while energetically scraping away you may hit one of these holes and rip the skin, sometimes damn near in two. That's one sure way to take the thrill out of working skins. It can ruin one's whole day, believe me.

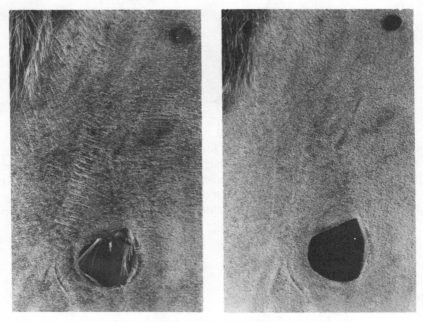

LEFT: Hair side dehaired. RIGHT: Sanded and ready.

When I get to dehairing I move at a pretty fast pace but I WATCH EACH AND EVERY STROKE OF THE SCRAPER. The hair comes off easily. The epidermis, which must also be removed (to allow the brains to penetrate) is not always as easy. Scrape every inch of the skin until certain that all of the epidermis is off (very seldom is it ever entirely removed). If you closely study the skin as you go, you will be able to see the epidermis. It is not a solid sheet like the membrane on the flesh side. It is more like a sandpaper coating. Though it can be seen on any part of the skin, it is most apparent at the flanks and other thinner areas. If the epidermis has ANY moisture in it at all it will be about impossible to remove. The areas where the hair is the thickest (such as the forward part of the flanks and the butt end) will be the last parts of the skin to dry completely. In these areas I have been known to scrape VERY LIGHTLY WITH A VERY SHARP BLADE to remove the hair only, going back later to remove the epidermis with either the scraper or sandpaper. Damp epidermis is rubbery. It won't work. You'll only tear the skin if you try.

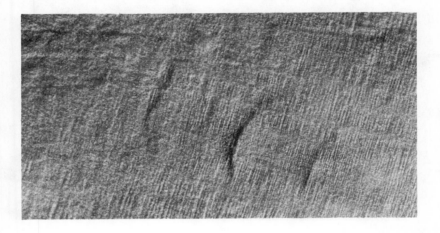

Three scores seen from hair side...ready for sanding.

When I am finished dehairing I have been over every square inch of the skin. I know that the epidermis is removed and that any ridges created while scraping have been smoothed with the scraper. Now go over the entire surface with sandpaper as done on the other side. CAUTION--It is possible to sand completely through a skin...go tenderly at thinner areas. Sometimes at the flanks, but especially at the scores, it may be best to leave some of the epidermis, going over it lightly with sandpaper only to break it up enough for the brains to penetrate. You will have to feel a lot of this out and do what seems right.

31

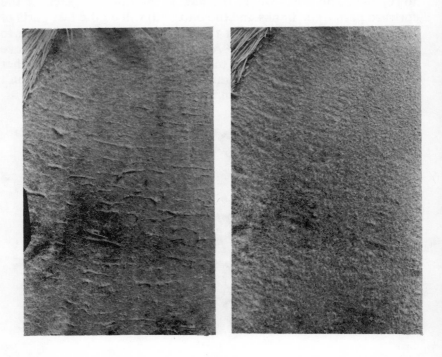

Hair side at flank. Note remaining epidermis at left. Right photo shows
sanded and ready for brain.

BRAINING

What needs to be done now is to get the oils of the brain into every pore and fiber of the skin. This is the easiest and fastest step of the operation.

The primary sources of brain (if not from the critter from whom we've taken the skin) are slaughter houses, butchers or the local market. I find it most convenient to purchase them by the pound, packed in your basic primitive plastic container, from the local supermarket. They cost a bit more than a dollar per pound and that's plenty enough to do one skin. You should not use less than a pound as it needs to be mixed with a certain volume of water.

Take your pound of brain and beat them thoroughly with an egg beater, blender, etc. Add just a little water, maybe a cup, and beat away. You can get by just squishing it with your hands. The object is to liquify the brain as much as possible. Now add this to approximately ¾ - 1 gallon of water, bring to a boil and simmer until greyish white, about 10-15 minutes. Let this cool until just comfortably warm to your hand.

With a large paintbrush, sponge, etc., apply this solution to both sides of the skin. You don't need to be too liberal with the brain solution now. You just need to get the skin pliable enough to cut from the frame and fold easily into the bucket. Fold the now pliable skin into the bucket of brain solution and work it with your hands for several minutes. With some of the smallest, thinnest skins, this is all that would be necessary. But I have never yet let any skin get by with only one soaking in the brains. I have had too many skins not receive a deep enough penetration of the brain and this won't be discovered until you have spent several hours working the skin and suddenly wind up with a stiff product...and then have to return to this stage. That's a lot of extra work that can be easily prevented with very little effort now. There is no special time limit that the skin has to be left in the brain. Once you have complete penetration you are ready to finish it out. The shortest time for very small skins would be about 15-20 minutes with two soakings.

With some of the thicker, larger skins, it works well to apply several coats of the brain before cutting from the frame. Each coat should be allowed to dry, preferably in the sun, and then either scraped or sanded before applying the next coat.

Between soakings the skin must be wrung to remove as much moisture as possible. As mentioned before, the skin will draw water like a sponge. Brain, being a solid matter and the oils being thicker than water, will not be absorbed into the skin as readily as water. With the thinner areas this is no problem, one soaking is enough. The thicker areas though will require additional soakings. We must get all the water out of the skin that we possibly can so that when it is re-immersed into the solution the water will not only bring more brain with it but will also draw what is already there ever deeper.

The wringer from an old wringer washer works just fine for this. Run the skin through this several times.

The traditional way, and the way that I did all of mine until I found the wringer, is to drape the skin around a small tree limb (or the lariat stretched tightly) overlapping it by about ⅓ and rolling and folding the skin onto and into itself, tucking in all loose ends until it is tightly rolled together. The accompanying photos show this better than I could every hope to describe it. Place a solid stick (approximately 1'' in diameter) through the opening and twist the skin until tight...pull...twist some more and then pull some more. The moisture will run and drip out (place the bucket to catch the drippings). This will take only a coupla minutes. Now stretch the skin as open as you can get it and repeat. After the second wringing, open and stretch the skin over the rope to really open the fibers up as much as possible. Pull in all directions. This will allow the brain better penetration upon re-immersion. Return the skin to the solution. Repeat this process until you are certain of complete penetration. The average 10 sq. ft. skin should be put through this process 4-5 times. YOU CANNOT GET TOO MUCH BRAIN INTO THE SKIN - BUT YOU MAY NOT GET ENOUGH.

After the final braining, wring the skin a few extra times to remove all possible moisture.

You will find this is the only stage in the process that really attracts flies. If a fresh skin is used, the fleshing process is not smelly but flies really are attracted to brain.

ABOVE LEFT: Wringing excess moisture from skin by hand before (ABOVE RIGHT) putting it around rope and overlapping by about ⅓ and (BELOW LEFT) rolling it into itself and (BELOW RIGHT) inserting stick and twisting.

Wringing out every bit of moisture.

SEWING OF HOLES

Holes. Every skin has a hole...or two...or three...or more. Some big, some little, and now is the time to do something about them. I have waited until I was finished with the tanning but then end up with patches, which don't really look all that bad but are more trouble and time consuming than what we will do now. At this point I use artificial sinew for the thread. Later, when I finish it out, I re-do them with real sinew. Any strong thread will work at this point but it must be strong enough to withstand the stretching and rubbing that the skin will endure from now on. Most holes, except bullet holes, will lie in some particular direction. Sew them in the direction that they lie. Whip stitch the hole shut and tie off twice. The skin will be abused from now on so make them good tight stitches. Poorly sewn holes will tear out and weak thread will break. In addition to all holes, sew the thinner scores shut as they will invariably tear also. Do all of the sewing from the former flesh side as the hair side will be used as the outside of any finished product.

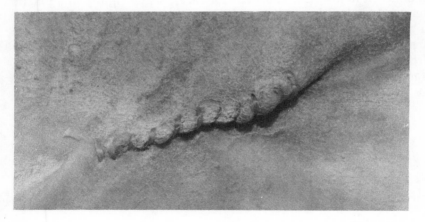

Hole sewn prior to finishing. Puckers will be eliminated while stretching.

Most skins have some form of scar tissue from old wounds. The most common are the long "scrapes" running down the center of the back made when going under barbed wire fences. Scrape these some with the small blade of a knife. Sometime you can get rid of them, sometimes not.

You will also often find larger areas of scar tissue; a result of a more serious wound to the deer in the past. Cut them out now and sew the hole shut. If these don't completely tear out as the skin is worked, they will dry hard. A single seam shows less and is easier to do than a patch. After the stretching and working of the skin which follows, all puckers now apparent will be eliminated. You can leave the holes sewn as is when finished though often times there will be stiffness where the stitches are. I re-sew with sinew. Usually the hole will have to be elongated slightly when this is done to eliminate the pucker.

If there are many holes that require considerable time to sew, the edges of the skin may begin to dry too much and stiffen and you may be required to add more moisture. This normally can be accomplished simply by wringing it one more time which will disperse the moisture already in the skin.

Many times at this point, if I want to delay the next step, I will only stretch the skin once completely around to open the pores and then roll it in towels (to absorb moisture), seal it tightly in a plastic bag and put it either in the refrigerator or freezer. It can be left for a coupla days like this in the refrigerator or indefinitely in the freezer. If left too long in the refrigerator it will sour and rot. The freezer has the additional advantage of ice crystals helping somewhat in opening and stretching the fibers.

FINISHING

At this point if we were to throw the skin out on the ground or over a limb, in a coupla hours it would shrink to a fraction of its size and become quite hard. Our purpose now is to prevent this from happening. There are a number of methods of working the skin soft but I will cover only the one I presently use as I find this is the easiest. With this method, at any point during the drying process the skin can be rolled as mentioned before and placed in the refrig/freezer.

The weather does, of course, affect how quickly the skin dries. My personal preference is a slow drying day over a hot, windy one. A fast drying skin can be hell to keep up with.

What we have to do now is to keep the fibers of the skin from doing what they want naturally to do...shrink and pull together as they dry. For this we will pull and stretch the skin around the lariat all the time that it is drying. I have read one account of a Navaho method of using hands and feet to do the stretching and have done so successfully on smaller skins in by the fire during the winter. As I have said, many methods work. All methods have one thing in common...to keep every fiber in the skin stretched and open to its fullest while drying. Without the addition of the brain (oils), the rawhide would still dry stiff, though not as stiff as if not stretched. The addition of the oils allows the individual fibers to pull apart and actually swell and soften as they dry...but we must keep each and every fiber stretched to its fullest the entire time that the skin is drying. (The above action of the brain is not scientific fact, just my observations and the easiest way that I know to describe what's taking place).

Tie one end of the lariat to the base of a tree and the other to a limb about six feet up and pull it tight. The skin is now draped around the rope and pulled in all directions the entire time that it is drying. Begin at the neck and grab a handful of skin and really lay into it. You needn't worry about the thicker parts of the skin tearing. Lean back and use your entire body weight. Hand over hand work your way all the way down the skin to the rump...then turn it half way and begin pulling the other direction (lengthways)...and repeat...and repeat...and repeat.

When pulling the thinner edge areas, such as the flanks, take

TOP: Holding skin in 6-8 inches from
edges and stretching hard.
BOTTOM: A second grip at the
thinner edge and a little lighter pull.

two handholds..one in about 6-8 inches where the skin is thicker and pull like hell and another grip at the edge with a little lighter pull. This insures that the heavier central portions get enough stretching and in the process you don't overdo and rip through at the thinner edge.

At any point the skin may be rolled in towels and placed in the refrig/freezer. As it becomes drier the towels may be omitted and

When stretching...really lay into it.

41

the remaining moisture allowed to disperse upon the skin.

Now a major time and effort saver, a tip gleaned from a fellow tanner at the '85 NAPR Western. "Why", says he, "take the extra time and effort to roll the skin in towels and refrigerate? If you've got the time to work it out, just throw it out onto the ground and let it air dry for 10 to 20 minutes. Then stretch it open again...and repeat until dry".

Well, I thought, if that does work, and no reason for it not to, I'd better give it a try.

The next skin that I did was an average 10 sq. footer and I tried it...IT WORKS! And what a time and effort saver. It took about 3½ hours for me to finish that skin out but only about half that time was spent stretching. However one must use caution not to let the skin overdry while not being worked...otherwise, back to the brain solution. The idea is to allow only a certain amount of the moisture to evaporate (at the same time the skin will shrink proportionately) and to open up the fibers by stretching before any portion of the skin has dried beyond the point where you are able to easily stretch and soften it. Keep a close watch on it. And if something comes up and you want to quit, wrap and refrig/freezer it.

You should also put the remaining brain solution in the fridge before it sets in the warm too long...it will sour in a hurry. You can use it on another skin or you may even have to use it yet again on this one if you haven't gotten complete penetration. I have used the same solution, with the addition of more brain and water, on as many as ten skins...but that's just being cheap. Fresh solution seems to work better.

At this point I think of the skin at 3 stages-wettest-medium-dry. In the wettest stage, the skin will spend more time on the ground than on the rope. The midpoint of drying is the more critical stage and more time will be spent stretching/rubbing. When pretty sure that the skin is dry and you are just ascertaining the fact, less time can again be spent on the rope.

At about the time the thinner areas are drying out, concentrate your efforts on the thicker neck, back and ham areas.

This is also the stage where the term "sweat and blood" pertains. Unconditioned knuckles will blister and bleed. Bandages over the first knuckle joint and/or tight fitting rubber gloves with fingertips cut off help. Time will toughen them.

42

Begin rubbing the skin around the rope while stretching as soon as it dries enough to do so easily. This helps to crush and stretch the fibers, raises the nap to a fluffier texture and the friction helps to speed the drying process somewhat. Rub with vigor.

Don't quit until you are positive that the skin is dry. Any little bit of moisture will detract from a number one piece of buckskin. Don't forget that as long as there is any moisture left in the skin at all it will shrink and stiffen as it dries. If you stayed with it, the average 10 sq. ft. skin will take approximately 3½ to 4 hours to finish out.

The finished buckskin will be a creamy white in color and soft and fluffy as the best of flannel. But...if this fine piece of material were allowed to get wet (and remember this will seem to draw moisture as brain and other things will draw flies) you will find yourself back to where you were four hours ago...if allowed to dry naturally it will shrink and stiffen. So though we have a fine piece of buckskin, we are certainly not finished with it. It makes no sense to make clothing or bags if we can't really use it.

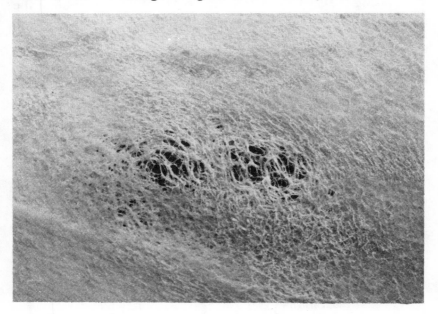

If I was limited to only one photo to illustrate this book this would be it. This is the detail of the fibers that we are working with.

43

SMOKING

What we do now is smoke the skin. As with the oils of the brain, we need to penetrate smoke into every fiber of the now soft buckskin. I have heard of various things this does to the skin but as of this date I don't really know truthfully what it does do. I do know it works and it is a necessary step to end up with a useful piece of material that will dry soft (or will require only a minimum of rubbing) after a good wetting.

The old way of smoking skins is to sew it into a cone from the neck to the rump, leaving the rump open. Into a hole in the ground (approximately 6" in diameter x 18" deep) place hot coals to a depth of 6-8" and cover with punky wood. What is wanted is a smudge of dense, warm smoke. Stake the open end of the skin over the smudge and tie the neck area to a low tree limb or a tripod. Smoke can also be piped to the hanging skin a number of feet making it easier to control the fire/smoke and eliminate the possibility of scorching the skin. It is a good idea to also sew a piece of material, such as denim or canvas, to the bottom of the skin (additional security against scorching). Keep the skin open so that the warm dense smoke can penetrate overall. When one sees the discoloration of the smoke seeping through the thinner areas

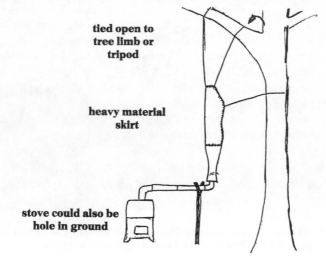

tied open to
tree limb or
tripod

heavy material
skirt

stove could also be
hole in ground

the skin is then inverted and smoked as well from the other direction. This is certainly the quickest way to smoke one, or just a few, skins. Not including the sewing and set-up time, the actual smoking is from 15-30 minutes per side, depending on how dark a shade is desired. This method actually forces the smoke through the skin whereby in the next method the smoke is absorbed by exposure and therefore takes considerably more time for complete penetration. I very seldom use this method as it requires one's constant attention and I normally have a number of skins to smoke at a time. I have read and been told that the smoke has to be warm to accomplish its mission. Cold smoke apparently won't work. Myself, I've never tested the cold smoke story.

I smoke 99% of my skins in a tipi. I have used a small shed before which is fine for pelts or individual skins but too small for any quantity of skins. I know of some who place the stove used right in the lodge. This is inconvenient to my way of thinking as you must burn the coals outside and then transport to the stove to avoid scorching the skins. It's also much easier to tend the smudge in the smokefree out-of-doors. I place my 18' lodge next to a ledge, put the stove below and pipe the smoke about 12 ft. to the center of the lodge. I also put a rain cap on the end of the pipe to help disperse the rising smoke which leads towards more consistant coloring of the skins.

Tie the skins to the uppermost part of the poles. I run a piece of heavy thread through the edge of the skin with a needle and then tie it around the poles loose enough to hang free so that all parts are exposed to the smoke. They could also be tacked to the poles. Either very long legs or a step ladder is necessary. With this method you can hang 8-12 skins, depending upon the size of both skins and lodge, and all will come out the same shade and color. After closing the smoke flaps tight as for a storm, with liner in place, put a towel or two in the crotch formed by the poles to slow the escape of the smoke as much as possible.

Prior to hanging the skins, build a large fire in the stove using a hard wood to hold long lasting coals. Oak is my favorite...charcoal will suffice. Remember to disconnect the pipe. By the time that the skins are hung and the lodge closed tight, the coals should be about right. Replace the pipe so as to heat it quickly to create a good draft and then almost immediately cover the coals with fine shredded punky wood. The rottenest, most punky wood that you can find is the best. Don't confuse soft, wet wood with rotten, punky. If wet when gathered, spread it out to dry. The wood needs to be punky and unburnable to create the dense smoke that is necessary. We don't need to add moisture by burning wet stuff. I have tried using green wood but it burns even hotter than the dry oak and we don't want straight heat to possibly scorch the skins. A combination of punky cottonwood and red cedar sawdust leaves my skins a light, bright, lively tan. The same combination used in the first method of forcing the smoke through, is much darker and

Smoke piped to tipi from stove
placed below ledge.

46

not nearly so lively. The choice of woods will dictate the final coloring.

A number of skins hanging in tipi for smoking.

I begin this project early in the morning on a day when no rain is expected in the immediate future. Rain will always enter the lodge at the apex and run down the poles and a chance is always being taken when one hangs a dozen unsmoked skins in the lodge. A sudden squall would create havoc. By hanging them early in the a.m. of a clear day, I can begin the actual smoking before 8 a.m. and by the time that I quit for the day at about 10 p.m., I feel secure that if it does rain during the night enough smoke has penetrated so a bit of moisture won't hurt. I would, though, have the skins cut down and in the house at the first hint of a storm within the first day and a half of smoking.

In order to keep a steady, heavy cloud rising from the stove, you will have to stir the coals every 20 minutes or so and keep adding more punk when necessary. Every two to three hours you will also need to rebuild the fire for more coals. Do not forget to disconnect the pipe when doing this.

I follow this process for three 12-14 hour days while working on other skins only a few feet from the stove. Late in the afternoon of the third day I remove the skins, soak them in cold well water and hang them from the clothesline. Most that I've read on the smoking of skins says to place them in a sack overnight to allow the smoke and color to set. I don't do this and have had no ill effects with my results. After the skins have dried I pull and rub each one by hand to insure that the smoke has done its job, and then let them air for a number of days.

That's it. You now have a fine piece of buckskin that's worth $10 or more a square foot. More than that, you have the satisfaction of having taken a raw piece of material from nature (no kit here) and by your own labors have created a fine, beautiful, useful finished product...something that you can point to and honestly proclaim with pride, "I MADE THIS".

Because of numerous requests, I'm adding this "hair-on" supplement as of the 4th printing.

Leaving the hair on when brain tanning requires the application of a few different rules. The skin (pelt, hide, whatever) should not be soaked in the brain solution as with buckskin...this can result in hair slippage. The brain should be painted on the former flesh side, allowed to dry, the dried brain "film" scraped off and then repeated until you are certain that you have COMPLETE penetration. Remember that you are penetrating from only one side and where with the same thickness buckskin that might require 8 applications (soakings/wringings), you will here require more than twice that number. Thinner pelts (fox, cats) might get by with only 1 or 2 applications (I would do 4-5 at least...remember that you cannot overbrain). The thickest, toughest PELT that I have done is the beaver. After successfully doing five extra large/blanket size ones, I wouldn't hesitate to apply the solution as many as 40-50 times...lots of work but the fine finished results were well worth the effort. (I can do a coupla buckskins in the time that it takes to do a larger beaver). The beaver I skin "open" and stretch round on a willow hoop, etc. I lace it using needle and artificial sinew (waxed nylon) thread, about 1 inch apart. Lace it with the holes pretty close to the edge and be especially careful around the face....what we are trying to do is save all that we can. I prefer to work all other pelts "case" skinned. The dried pelt can be kept on the stretcher for the brainings. When the legs are left on, I staple them open to thin slats...I skin the paws as open as I can and soak them in the brain (they should be "tanned", but I know nothing of that...I only do things the natural way...soaking in the oils of the brain can't hurt.) Ears should be skinned out as much as possible...to the tip. I also soak these. All meats and fats must be removed from these areas or they will eventually rot, if gotten wet, and the hair will then slip. The final coat of brain can be applied, applied, applied. Saturate it as much as you can...then maybe place a warm, damp towel (damp with brain solution is fine) on the flesh side, place it in a plastic sack and allow it to sit until as pliable as when green (don't overdo it...it could begin to rot and cause hair slippage)...and then work it over the rope or by hand until dry and soft.

Deer with the hair on, I wouldn't even bother with brain tanning. The hollow hairs of the deer break off if you even look hard at it...the only practical use for a hair on deer is for a wall hanging...and then it doesn't need to be soft. I have done one deer robe. No more. It is nice, but you can't do anything with it but pick up hairs wherever you might visit...eventually ending up with a piece of buckskin anyhow...it's just not worth the extra work...**and it is a lot of extra work.** I have read where Indians just threw the raw skin on the floor of the lodge...and when the hair all fell out, they had a softened piece of rawhide ready to brain into buckskin. One that you wanted for a wall hanging could be saturated with pure neatsfoot oil (for better penetration), or brained and only worked semi-soft.

But if you insist...and also for elk, buffalo, etc. Here are just some tips to kinda help you along.

Follow the preparation steps up to page 28 in this book ..now I'm not talking about skins or hides with the legs or faces left on...I would now begin to paint the brain solution on, scraping between coatings as with the pelts. Apply, apply, apply....you can't do too much. YOU will have to judge as to how many coatings each will need. Finally, lay the frame out flat and apply the brain until the skin is saturated...(you might even repeat this several times)....and when pliable as when green, DO NOT cut it from the frame...there will be too much bulk for you to work over a rope...Stand the frame up, and beginning with a canoe paddle (or something similar), begin to run this down the hide....you will be stretching the hide and at the same time squeegeeing the moisture out...you will only be working the flesh side...the epidermis will restrict the stretching process...you will work your butt off...but keep at it. You **must** until it is dry and soft. As the hide gets drier, graduate to a smaller sized stick to stretch with (a rounded down ax handle will work well)...about here you will begin to wish that you hadn't begun this project...it is a "buster"...but worth it. Someone once showed me an old photo of Indian women "playing" by bouncing children up and down on a buffalo hide like a trampoline...playing, hell, they were stretching the hide soft. Whichever way you decide to do this, it must be continued until it is completely finished...no half hour breaks here... For this project it would be best to have one or more helpers. If you have properly prepared the surface and applied enough brain to achieve COMPLETE penetration...and if you keep the proper stretching up until it is completely dry...you will end up with a fine robe.

It is best to smoke the finished pelt or robe in a smoke house or in the tipi...especially if the legs and face are left on it will be about impossible to sew into a bag.

This is only a quickie jotting of notes for hair-on brain tanning -- far from complete -- but used in conjunction with this book you should be able to end up with a fine product.

SEWING WITH SINEW

Assuming that for the most part the people reading this are those either involved in buckskinning or just interested in a more natural way of life, I want to show how to use another completely natural product for threads when turning your buckskin into ʳlothing or whatever.

Sinew, on a critter, is tendon. Critter, in our case, is most likely a deer. On our critter we have two sources of convenient, useable sinew...the tendons of the legs and the loin sinew, of which there are two flat strips, one lying on either side of the backbone on top of the meat.

The leg tendons are shorter and more difficult to work into threads and since I have no first hand experience working with it I'll cover only the more easily workable loin sinew.

Elk loin sinew will run a little over two feet in length...buffalo closer to three. Deer sinew, which I mostly use, runs about 15-18 inches long and is finer than the other two. Sinew can be obtained from some buckskinning supply houses. I know of one source which charges $6.75 per strip for deer and I have bought elk strips

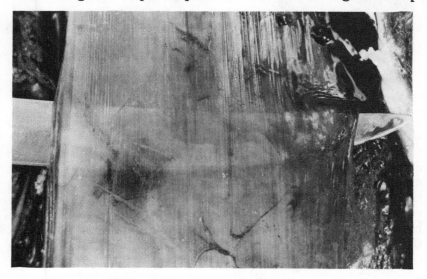

DULL knife run under tendon while attached to deer

for $7.50 at rendezvous. A single strip contains a hearty supply of threads.

I obtain all of my deer sinew directly from the critter. Though not a difficult chore, when deer are usually available to me the temperature has a tendency to be well below the freezing mark and since working with bare hands makes the job of removal much easier it can be mighty uncomfortable. The sinew cannot be removed from a frozen carcass.

Final scraping clean of strip. Bottom has been pulled loose from carcass while the top remains attached.

Most times the sinew is available from a deer whose skin is also obtainable. After skinning, make a cut up against and parallel to the backbone about ¼" deep. With your fingers, pull away the outer layer of fat and expose the silvery sinew lying atop the meat and running from the shoulder to the hip, 1-2 inches wide and tapering. Take a dull knife, a butter knife works well, and about midway in length run this under the sinew and begin working the blade in either direction separating the meat from the sinew. CAUTION: Too sharp a blade will cut the tendon. Clean the strip only to where it enters the hip, or goes into the shoulder, whichever way you're working...leave it attached to the carcass and clean it the other way. When separated the entire length-but still attached at the ends-continue to run the knife back and forth several times to get the strip as clean as possible. Remove all meat and fat. When this is as clean as you can get it, begin to work the knife into the hip until it pulls free at that end and then remove from the shoulder. You will need to cut somewhat into the meat at the ends to obtain the entire strip. Once loose from the critter, again scrape both sides until completely clean and then lay it out on a flat surface to dry. When you buy loin sinew from a source, this is what you will get.

The dried loin sinew strip.

Getting individual threads from this is easy. Take the strip and grab it between thumb and forefinger of each hand, close together, and work the sinew back and forth and round and round for a few seconds. This will break the strip into individual threads. Do this the entire length and you will have a real conglomeration of threads which can be stripped off as needed in the thickness desired. Thicker threads for sewing soles to moccasins...medium threads for general purpose garment and bag sewing and fine delicate threads necessary for quill or bead work. These finer strands are the most difficult to work loose in any length but with a bit of care and patience it can be done.

Sinew is surprisingly strong as it must be to have sufficed as bowstrings for the very powerful plains sinew-backed bow. It is certainly as strong as most of our modern day threads.

Threads can be pulled off individually as needed or many made up in advance. When making them in advance I find it easier to separate them if the strip is wetted first (after having broken threads apart).

Breaking threads loose by twisting in fingers.

Entire strip broken (took about three minutes)

Towards the middle of the strip, at the edge, begin to work the fibers free in the thickness desired. As this is worked loose you will find that towards the wide end of the strip the thread will be somewhat thicker than at the other. This is the forward end of the thread. When separated wet the thread, I use my mouth, until soft and lay it on a flat surface to dry. When ready to begin sewing, wet the thread thoroughly as before and thread the thick end through a needle (a glovers needle works best) and go to it. Before the availability of the needle the Indians would let the thicker end dry and that would stiffen enough to suffice as a needle through a hole punched with an awl. You will discover that with brain tanned skins you will not require a thimble.

Instead of a knot at the end of the thread, sew through the material once and then again to create a loop through which you will wrap (tie) the thread three times and then pull tight. Let about ¾ inch of the tail of the thread lie in line with your stitching and sew it under as you go. As the sinew dries it will shrink slightly and stiffen, conforming to the stitching, creating a tight knot and seam. Pull the stitches as tight as possible. When the thread breaks you will know that it is too tight. When you reach the end of one thread, tie it off as you began...a loop and wrapped three times...pull tight and let the end of the thread run in line with and under the next stitches.

Separated threads ready for use.

When the end of the seam is reached, tie the thread off twice, just in case. Then take the needle and run the thread "through" the center of the buckskin for about an inch and cut it off (try this with commercially tanned leather). Take the rounded butt end of your scissors, or something similar, and flatten the seams. Of course, all seams are sewn inside out. As mentioned before, all sewing with brain tan is on the former flesh side...the former hair side being the outside.

When finished, the seams will hardly be visible, the knots are almost indistinguishable and there are no loose threads.

By using sinew the user is just one more step up on the modern technological world of today. Another small step towards self fulfillment and sufficiency. And an otherwise fine piece of workmanship in your finished product gains a bit more value with just the slightest bit of extra effort.

Smoked skins hanging from line.

56

2

Primitive

Fire & Cordage

INTRODUCTION

The learning of the necessary "skills" to live directly with nature, eliminating the need of middlemen, is really not all that difficult. You learn a little about this aspect...a bit about that...and then another. Pretty soon you find that most of them overlap and that the further you get along in your natural education, the easier it is to learn.

Many years ago when I first got serious about putting all of this together (my first step was to get rid of the T.V....then electricity), I felt that if I was to learn a few of the basic primitive "survival" skills, I would really become quite the woodsman. I soon found that the more that I learned, <u>the more I still had to learn.</u>

I read...(and urge anyone interested in learning to also)... everything that I can lay my hands on that deals with living WITH nature. There is a lot written on all aspects of it. Some poor...some superb...but most lying somewhere in the middle. Before you can decide what is workable, you will have to get out and work with it...reading only goes so far. When you actually begin to put into practice what you are reading, then it becomes obvious just who knows what he or she, is writing about.

There is no "special talent" needed here...just a bunch of natural rules (physics) to follow. Any of the primitive skills, today as well as yesterday, can be carried to the extreme...and become an art. I am capable of taking flint, chert, obsidian or whatever rock, and turning it into a "functional" tool. I have seen the work of others at this...finely crafted blades of 8-10 inches, 1/4" thin...truely spectacular pieces of art. Work such as this has a tendency to scare away the ones interested in learning to knap flint. It shouldn't. To be functional, you need only to know how to throw one rock against another and to pick up the piece that will do the job at hand. (This book has nothing at all to do with the knapping of flint...just using this as a teaching aid).

I am far from being an expert on woodsmanship. I have, though, taught myself what I need to know to go naked into the wilderness and, not only survive, but before long to be living fairly comfortably (if I wasn't to freeze to death first). I refer to my teachings as primitive "living" skills...not "survival" skills,

It will be no more difficult for you to learn to apply
the lessons put forth here than it was for me to
learn to run the computer that put it here.

59

though they can be used in that concept. I have taught myself to be proficient in these skills...not an artist. When I wrote my book on brain tanning, I had tanned just over 100 skins. Others speak of their first 100. Those are the artisans. The same is true with this book. I have made hundreds of fires with the bow/drill...but not more than a coupla dozen with the hand drill methods. BUT, I am proficient enough in this to teach it to others. The same holds true with the making of cordage. I only a year ago got serious about learning this...but now am capable enough to teach it. The more you learn, the more that you realize what there is to learn...but it also is much easier to learn it.

The learning and practice of most primitive skills can be done in your backyard, garage, basement, even living room (depending on the wife or husband). You CAN become proficient in them without ever venturing beyond these bounds. And if ever in a primitive situation, either by choice or chance, though you will find that the application is not as easy as your back yard, you will still have the understanding and "feel" of the basic functions, the confidence that you "know" how to apply the various methods and you will own that special feeling of freedom that comes from knowing that you need "depend" on no other man.

February 1987

BOW/DRILL

The basic principle of making fire with either the bow or hand drill is really very simple...the amount of practice to develop that "special touch" to enable one to succeed in this on a regular basis is another thing.

To say "make fire" with the bow or hand drill is really a misnomer...actually what is accomplished is that the wooden drill spinning on another piece of wood creates friction...which creates dust...and eventually things get hot enough that a spark is created. The compressed pile of dust that has been formed becomes like the hot tip of a cigarette.THAT, is placed into a pile of tinder and coaxed into a flame.

Simple?...yeh, really it is. I have had students "make fire" within minutes of being exposed to this procedure...AND understand just what they were doing.

I'm first gonna show you how to "make fire" (bow drill first...hand drill a little later). I'll quickly show the necessary components and the steps to follow. THEN we'll get down to brass tacks and go through it again dwelling a bit more on how to assemble the parts and to put it all together. When you finish with this, you will be able to "make fire".

We have, of course, (1) the bow--a limber stick about 30" long...(2) the drill (3) the fireboard (both of which are soft woods) and (4) a cup (bearing block) in which the upper end of the drill is placed to keep it from drilling through the palm of your hand. The bowstring (5) will be covered in greater detail later in this book.

SIMPLIFIED:

We take a knife and cut a notch and a slight depression into the fireboard, twist the drill into the string of the bow, place one end of the drill into the depression of the fireboard, place the bearing block on top of the drill and spin the drill by pushing the bow back and forth until a spark is formed. We finish by dropping the spark into a prepared "birdsnest" of tinder and

(preceding page) The day most of these photos were shot, the temperature was in the 40's and it was misting. I threw up the crude shelter using only what one would normally have...two light jackets and a shirt, utilizing also rocks and grass. The purpose of the shelter was only to block the wind and rain from preventing my making of fire.

gently blowing it into flame. Easy?...sure. And you might be able to make it work with no more information that this. Thirteen years ago, three of us spent the better part of a day wearing ourselves out with no more information than what you have just

Raw squirrel skin cord "made fire" the first time. The hair rubbed off while in use...spark was found beneath pile of hair. Note thinness where skin is about break...fortunately I got the spark first (note coal) and also had plenty of extra length to re-use the skin after drying.

read...and made fire.

So now, I'm gonna go into a lot more detail about all of the "parts"...the whats and the whys, how to gather and make them under primitive conditions. The "special touch" you will have to develop yourself through practice...(it does come pretty easily).

BOW - the easiest piece to obtain. A reasonably limber stick (limb, piece of brush, etc.), 1/2-3/4" thick approximately 30" long. It needs to be limber enough to create just the "right amount" of tension on the string when the drill is inserted. Too limber and you will have trouble with the string slipping on the drill..too stiff and too much stress is placed on the string and the drill resulting in the drill continually flying out on you, and most often the breaking of the string. (The stress created on the string and the drill is nothing compared to the stress that will be building in you at this point.) The length of about 30" is also important (a bow of only a few inches or one of several feet would work...just not as well). At this length the bow is not too cumbersome and allows FOR A GOOD FULL SWEEP OF THE ENTIRE LENGTH...important....every time that the bow stops to change directions, everything cools off just a little...thus impeding your efforts.

Methods of nocking bow.

(left) One end of the bow I tie permanently, usually with a slip knot.
(right) The other end I tie with a single slip that can be untied easily and retightened as the string stretches. This is the end that I hold...this way I can also hold any long loose end to prevent it from flying around and possibly knocking my dust pile all to hell.

DRILL - We now need to be a bit more particular. A SOFT wood is necessary. Dead and dry (I'll mention damp wood later). Literally dozens of woods will work here. Cottonwood, aspen and yucca are my favorites...not only because they work well but also because they are available in abundance in the parts of the country where I live and travel. Willow is a favorite among many...I have heard that sage works well...box elder and hackberry. The smaller limbs and sapwood of cedar, locust and ash (the heartwoods of these are too hard). And the list goes on. I have been told and have read to avoid the resonous woods, such as pine...(but cedar works?)...experiment with what is available to you. Members of the cottonwood family (including birch, aspen, poplar) can be found in most parts of the country...they all work superbly). Search out dead limbs, preferably off the ground (to eliminate absorption of ground moisture), the bark weathered away. Check the condition of the wood by pressing it with your thumbnail...if it makes a slight indentation easily without crumbling, it should be about right. Also, if it breaks easily and cleanly with a snap it shows that it has no greenness or moisture left in it. The drill needs to be

A fresh drill (here yucca...my favorite combination is a yucca drill on a cottonwood fireboard). The right side is more pointed for the bearing block...the slight tit on the left helps it to stay where it belongs in the fireboard until the hole is enlarged.

about as big around as your little finger...or your thumb. No real exactness here, though I wouldn't go much for larger or smaller (the smaller drill spins more with each pass of the bow, thereby creating friction faster...but also drills through the fireboard faster...sometimes before the spark has formed). The

ength of the drill is from 6-8". Too long and it is hard to
_____e...too short and your bow hand gets in the way of the
drill and you can't see what is happening. And straight...if there
is a warp in the drill, it will wobble as it spins and create
problems. Most times a slightly curved drill can be straightened
with your knife.

FIREBOARD - The fireboard can, but need not be, the
same material as the drill. Usually though it will be. But again, it
must be a softwood. Check it's condition the same as for the
drill. The size of the board is variable. It need only be larger in
width than the diameter of the drill. I like to make mine from 1
1/2-2" wide (remember that nothing here is exact). Take the limb
of your choosing and with your knife, split it in half. Shave the
split side until the board will lay flat...shave down the round
side till the board is about 1/2" thick and then square up the
sides.

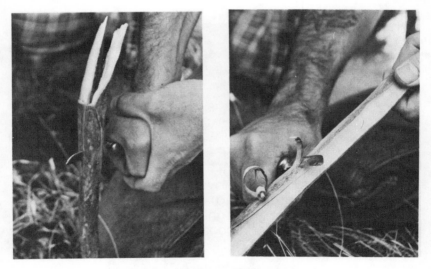

(left) splitting the fireboard.
(right) flattening and squaring the edges.

BEARING BLOCK - A very simple piece...very important...and not all that easy to come up with in a survival situation. For at-home work, I suggest a 1-oz. shot glass...it fits the hand comfortably...the hole is the right size for the drill and the surface is as smooth as you will find (eliminating friction). You can also find a semi-soft rock and drill a 1/2-3/4" hole in it-about 1/2" deep...lubricate it up with Crisco (bear grease in a can)...we need to eliminate the friction at this end...(I have in the past used various knots of hardwoods...some of those though have had soft spots in them and I was coming up with smoke from my palm before the fireboard). I carry with and use at home, demonstrations and in base camps a rock about 3x2 1/2x1 1/2" thick with a dandy hole in it...but it's pretty hefty to carry around in the timber. For now, this is all that you will need to know...we'll go into obtaining this under primitive conditions a bit later.

Since there is a definite satisfaction in taking your first ever spark created with the bow drill and blowing it into flame, let's have you gather up and prepare some TINDER at this time. If

Cedar bark stripped from tree (dead)

you can come up with a mouse or pack-rat nest, that is all that you will need. If not, then let's make one up. I really like the dry inner bark of cedar...cottonwood is good also..and some dry, fine grasses...roll these around in your hands until it is fine as a cotton ball. You won't need much. A small handfull will be plenty. Form a hole in it like a "birdsnest". Place this on a piece of bark or cardboard (so that when it bursts into flame you won't barbecue your hand).

67

Shredded between fingers (or rolled between palms) to loosen and separate fibers.

(left) birdsnest of cedar. (right) same of grasses.

With the information contained thus far, you are ready to "make fire". We'll run you through it once now. The information contained thereafter is certainly useful (or I wouldn't have gone to the trouble to write it), but deals mostly with gathering the materials under primitive conditions.

BOW - Archers, string your bow! Most any cordage will work...but it should be strong and not too thin...it will have a tendency to break easily with the first timer. Also, the heavier cordage (not rope) seems to get more of a grip on the drill. Here I would suggest using a "rawhide" (not really rawhide) boot lace...just about ideal. I twist mine tight...it seems to grab the drill just that much better. Just the "right amount" of tension you will begin to "feel" in short order. The string will stretch considerably with use, especially at first, and adjustments will have to be made as you go along. The bow is not strung tight...considerable slack is left. When the drill is placed in it, the slack is taken up (note photo) REMEMBER...the tension must be "just so"...too tight is worse than just a little slack...but there isn't much room for variables here.

Bow, in this case a piece of dogwood, strung with deer rawhide. I always string the drill the same way, resulting in the top of the drill being up and the drill ending up on the outside of the string, thereby staying out of the way of the bow hand.

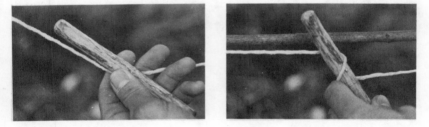

DRILL - Now let's take our selected piece for the drill. I like to point somewhat the upper end (end that goes into the bearing block), and when breaking in a new hole in the fireboard (as in this case), I find it easier to operate if I carve the working end into a slight tit (study photos here). By doing this, it has a tendancy to take a bit longer to "mate" the drill to the hole, but also assists in keeping the drill from kicking out of the fireboard while the depression enlarges to "fit" the drill...by the time the two "mate", the hole and drill fit better.

(left) Stick selected for drill. I chose the straight middle portion.
(right top) ...scoring around the stick first makes it easier to break (middle) where you want it to.
(bottom) "straightening" the drill by shaving it.

FIREBOARD - Now take ahold of the piece prepared for this. There are two approaches to take now. I'll talk you through one and mention the other. Both work.

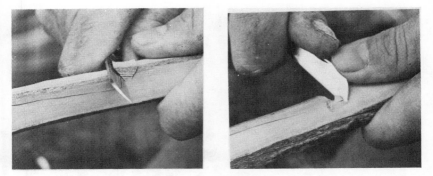

(left) cutting the notch and
(right) the depression for the drill.

With your knife, cut a "V" notch approximately 1/4 to 5/16" wide extending into the board MORE THAN ONE HALF THE DIAMETER OF THE DRILL...(note photos)...At the point of the "V" of this notch, dig out a slight depression for the end of the drill to fit. (the other method is to dig your depression first...then AFTER the hole has been started with the drill, to cut the notch). The depression MUST be in far enough so that when the hole is started, the notch retains enough material at the wide

part of the "V" (at the edge of the board) to prevent the drill from kicking out. If the drill does kick out, breaking off this retainer (which helps to hold the drill), you may as well begin a new hole as you will then encounter only frustruation.

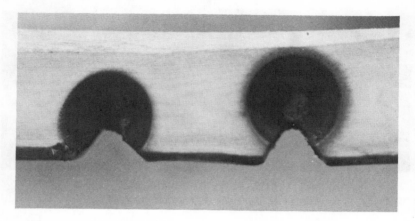

Hole on the left is too close to the edge...the drill will only fly out...when this happens, it is best to start another. The hole on the right is great. "V" could even be a little deeper, but this worked well.

Now, let's get serious. Place a piece of bark (you non-primitives can use cardboard), under the notch cut in the fireboard. This serves two purposes, (1) to catch the dust and spark enabling you to drop it into the tinder and (2) to act as an insulation between the fireboard/dust and the ground which may be damp, cool or both...in either case slowing down or preventing the creation of the spark.

The following instructions are for a right hander...you southpaws just reverse the procedure. Get down on your right knee. Place the ball of your left foot on the fireboard, making certain that it is secure and that it doesn't rock. An unsteady board can result in the knocking of your dustpile all to hell. I like the notch to be about 2 1/2-3" out from the inside of my foot...this is where my hand falls into place automatically DIRECTLY over the notch when my wrist is locked against my left calf. Wrap the drill in the string (as noted in photo) and place the proper end into the depression of the fireboard. Take the bearing block in your left hand, place it on the top of the drill,

Before you begin to "make fire", have all ingredients at hand. From left: fireboard, drill, bearing block, strung bow...tinder...four piles of kindling in various sizes and, at far right, larger wood...all layed out on my vest to keep it from absorbing ground moisture (the ground was wet.)

lock your left wrist SECURELY against your left calf (this is important-you want the hand holding the bearing block to be complete steady...if it sways to and fro while drilling, you will be inviting trouble). All that is necessary now is to run the bow back and forth. You will now have to start to develop the "feel" of what you are doing.

Drill straight up and down...left wrist locked securely against left calf.

The amount of downward pressure applied to the drill COMBINED with the speed of the bow is what determines how much friction is created, thus, how quickly a spark is formed. When you first begin, don't even think fire...concentrate only on becoming comfortable with the operation (kinda like chewing tobacco and walking at the same time). Make smooth, full strokes with the bow...run it the entire length of the string. Remember that everytime you change directions, that split second stop cools things off just a little. Keep the drill perpendicular.

The string has a tendency to want to wander either up or down the drill while it is spinning. This can be controlled by pointing the end of the bow either slightly up or down...whichever seems to work. The pressure that you are able to apply with your thumb and fingers of the bow hand on the string will also help.

Vary the amount of pressure on the drill. Begin with just a slight amount and increase it as you become more comfortable. Too much pressure and things have a tendency to want to bind up...and the string may begin to slip on the drill...whenever this happens you MUST let up on your pressure because no matter how fast the bow is moving, if the drill is not spinning there is no friction. If there isn't ENOUGH pressure applied, NOTHING will happen.

When begining to mate a new drill to a new hole (what we are doing here), there will be a certain amount of drilling where nothing seems to be happening. This can last from only several seconds to several minutes, depending on the type and the condition of the wood. At first the drill will spin SMOOTHLY....as if sliding on a freshly waxed floor. Then suddenly, as the drill and fireboard begin to "mate", it will act as if you have gone from the waxed floor to sandpaper...this difference you not only feel, but you can also hear.

NOW, control and feel become all important. The drill, which up to now was easy to control, suddenly becomes more difficult. You may find you need to slightly tilt the wrist holding the bearing block ever so slightly one way and then the other as you run the bow back and forth to keep the drill from kicking out of the hole.

Just after the two mate, and the first smoke and dust appear, I usually take a quick break before I go after the spark. This allows me to catch my breath and relax muscles so that when I start up again I am fresh...kinda makes things a bit easier.

At this point, bear in mind that the hole is not yet deep enough to "hold" the drill on it's own...it still takes some care on your part to keep it from kicking out...and now that the friction has begun, the drill is a bit more difficult to control. You will feel this out in short order. Vary the amount of downward pressure on the drill to coincide with the speed of the bow. YOU WILL DEVELOP THE FEEL.

Here, another VERY important tip. I had made fire this way for eleven years before stumbling onto this...and now I can't imagine ever having made fire successfully, regularly, without having applied it. As mentioned before, the string will stretch while in use...a good flexible bow will compensate for a lot of this...but eventually the string will become so loose that it slips on the drill when you apply the proper amount of pressure needed. One time, just as the spark was about ready, the string began slipping badly. Without thinking, I took the string between the first two fingers and the thumb of the bow hand and took up enough slack so that I was able to successfully finish. Now, anytime that I take up the bow, the fingers and thumb just naturally wrap on the string (note photo).

Note how I use my thumb and fingers to control string tension.
Use whatever is most comfortable for you.

If you concentrate on keeping the drill perpendicular, the left wrist locked tightly against the left calf, the bow taking long, smooth strokes, the fireboard steady and not wobbling, the spark will form of itself. First the smoke will begin...then dust...heavier smoke and the dust will get blacker...Keep yourself relaxed and just concentrate on the smoothness of the operation. There will be spark.

Once the drill and hole mate, the spark will normally be created in less than 30 seconds. Once, timing myself, I had spark in 10 seconds. If everything is working, it doesn't take long.

When you have your spark (it most times is hidden...the dust pile smoking is your sign), carefully lift away the drill and place it aside. There is no big rush. I have left the smoldering dust for up to four minutes while I went in search of tinder and still had a fine coal. Pick up the bark or cardboard holding the spark...fan it some with your hand...blow gently on it...let any slight breeze help (not a wind strong enough to blow it away). When it glows, drop it into your birdsnest of tinder. Fold the tinder over the top...and begin blowing the spark...more and more as it gets hotter. Suddenly...fire!

(left) note black dust and smoke...spark is there.
(right) dropping it into the "birdsnest" of tinder.

(left) blowing tinder to flame and (right) adding the first of the "finest" shavings of kindling.

(left) adding larger kindling and (right) larger pieces of wood. On wet days, the inside of most woods will be dry. From spark to good solid fire (this series of photos) took less than a minute, but to get the spark took longer than usual because of the wet weather and gusty winds.

When I first began making fire this way, I had the tendency to wear myself out by the time that the spark was formed. Someone else had to blow it into flame because I would just blow the whole damn thing away. No need for this. If one concentrates ONLY on the control of the drill and the smooth operation of the bow...taking extra care to remind oneself to remain calm and relaxed...the spark will form of itself and you are left fresh enough to easily blow the spark to flame. If you are winding yourself, you are doing something wrong.

Many times it seems that no matter what you do, a spark will just not come into being...the chances of this happening seem to rise proportionately with the size of the crowd that you are demonstrating this to.

But WHEN, not if, you do get that spark...the first or the hundredth, cherish and glow with it. It is something that I never take for granted. Like calling coyotes...there are so many things that can go wrong, each time it works I feel a real sense of accomplishment.

SOME OBSERVATIONS

For the last few passes of the bow (some say) apply slightly less pressure on the drill...to kick out the spark that may be under it. I usually don't find this necessary, but if unsure of the spark sometimes do it.

If I seem to have difficulty getting a sure spark, I will sometimes make several "furious" passes with the bow at the last. I don't like to do this though because it has the tendency to wind me...and at times I lose control of the operation at this point and the drill kicks out, knocking away the dustpile.

Usually you can tell that the spark has formed because you will see a wisp of smoke rising from the dust...separate from the smoke created by the drill.

On occassion, the entire pile of dust will suddenly glow...a good feeling.

A single hole in the fireboard is capable of many sparks. Before using it again it helps to roughen slightly the tip of the drill and the hole.

After several uses, especially with too tight a string, the drill will become "too round", causing the string to slip. This is usually easily corrected by carefully shaving it until it is once again "unround".

(upper) note how cordage has "rounded" drill
(lower) drill has been shaved "unround" and tip has
been formed for starting a new hole.

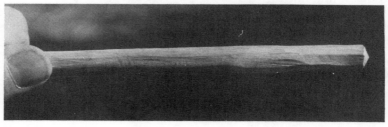

78

Ear wax, oil from your hair or the side of your nose, will help to eliminate friction in the bearing block...(always remember that you are eliminating friction at the bearing block...and creating it at the fireboard).

Avoid placing the wrong end of the drill into the fireboard...that little bit of oil can really foul things up.

Under damp conditions, find and use the driest woods available...and get into the driest location that you can to work..if the wood is only damp, it can still work..but it will take a lot longer...the spinning drill eventually will dry things enough to work..but you will have a lot against you.

Under primitive conditions, the hardest components to gather will be the string (covered later) and the bearing block. Sometimes you will find a ready made block in a stone with just the right depression..but don't count on it. You might find a piece of bone that will work (the skulls of small critters)...also look for a piece of HARD wood...possibly a knot with a slight hole that you can easily enlarge. If something is located that might work, the hole can be formed or enlarged by using the bow/drill...using a HARD piece of wood for the drill (or maybe you will be lucky enough to come up with a "natural" rock drill)...something harder than the block material. Ingenuity and common sense help a lot.

HAND DRILL

To now explain to you how to make fire with the hand drill will be simple...in theory. In practice, you will be faced with a much greater challange.

The basic principle remains the same -- to create friction with a wooden drill on a fireboard...the spinning of the drill, the fireboard, the notch, the dust and the spark...all kinda the same. But...

DRILL - the material for use here differs little from what we covered for the bow/drill...except because of the extra difficulty in creating friction here one should be more choosy. The ideal length of a hand drill, for my length arms, is just about 30"...I usually begin with a few inches longer as this shortens quickly. Too long of a drill and the top has a tendency to whip around, causing you to lose control (so much more important here). Too short and you don't get the full benefit of a long downward run of the hands before having to return to the top once again. I prefer a diameter of about 1/4" ... more revolutions of the drill per sweep of the hands(too thin and limber will cause the drill to bend from the downward pressure applied by the hands.)

Note last 1 1/2" of this cattail hand drill SLIGHTLY shaved to remove SOME, not all, of the outer shell.

FIREBOARD - Again, the basic is the same as for the bow/drill. I had been having trouble catching a spark, when someone suggested a fireboard thinner than that which I had been using. When I cut down the cottonwood board that I had been using to about 1/4", things improved. With the softer yucca I still keep the board about 1/2" thick. With the hand drill, I begin the depression and hole BEFORE I cut the notch. I also cut the notch slightly different than for the bow drill. I keep it closed at the top, flaring it open towards the bottom of the fireboard. (note photo) I find the drill has cut the hole below this

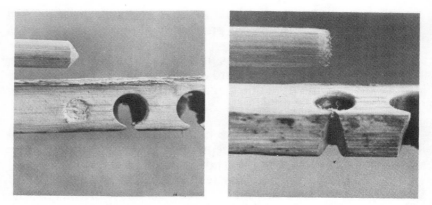

(left) Fresh cattail hand drill tip and depression in fireboard. (right) The hole begun. Note carefully how notch is cut. The cattail drill and yucca fireboard are my favorite for the hand drill.

point before things get hot enough to matter...and that the closed top then forces more of the HOT dust into the notch rather than letting it spill over the top.

To put this in action...get into a COMFORTABLE position. My left foot again holds the fireboard...but your position may, or may not be the same. For me, it's slightly different. I need to place the foot out a bit further and drop my knee out of the way somewhat so that I am able to get a good FULL run of my hands down the length of the drill. I use the side of my heel to hold the board. Your hands must come down STRAIGHT...You <u>must</u> keep the drill perpendicular. By placing my foot and knee slightly different than for the bow drill, I am able to start my hands "rubbing" at the highest comfortable point (in my case 30" and to keep them going to a point about 6" above the fireboard. Once reaching the lowest point, raise your hands again to the top ONE AT A TIME so that you are able to keep CONSTANT DOWNWARD PRESSURE on the drill...if any air is allowed to reach under the drill, it allows everything to cool off....once both hands are up, repeat the procedure. Eventually the smoke, dust and spark will appear...but not all that easily.

This procedure WILL wear you out. A completely new set of muscles are at work here...After you have done this for 45 seconds or so, you will feel as if you have run the Boston Marathon...using your arms instead of your legs. It is strenuous. It takes a lot of practice to get this operation down

SMOOTHLY...which it must be to be successful. I would suggest that you do a lot of practicing before you even think fire...this is a bit more complicated than chewing tobacco and walking...here you must also juggle. It does take practice...not only to get everything running smoothly, but also to get yourself into some semblance of physical well being...this do sap your energies. (Anyhow, it do mine). It also creates blisters on the palm of your hands...which evenually will turn to callouses if worked at long enough. It took me well over a month of daily workouts to develop a good set of callouses and a four week vacation of "city living" took them away.

When you first attempt this, I suggest going slow. Get the movements down to where everything runs smoothly and automatically. Your hands clasp the drill at the top...rub the drill between your palms, keeping CONSTANT downward pressure...keep the drill perpendicular...when your hands reach the bottom, grasp ahold of the drill with the thumb and forefinger of the left hand...raise the right to the top, holding it firmly while the left comes back up (thanx, Bob)...repeat...repeat...repeat. Over and over, slowly at first and then speed up as it becomes more natural to you. Speed and downward pressure are all important.

Spitting on your hands helps retain a little extra "grip" on the drill, (thanx, Bryan) allowing a few more spins before your hands reach bottom. Always put the thickest end of the drill down...this kinda slows the hands trip downward also.

My most commonly used drill is the stem of the cattail. (thanx, Dick) Most of these stalks are just slightly bent though...they must be straight, so be selective. I know of one woodsman who uses only willow here. Since an "ideal" drill is sometimes difficult to find, a good idea is to make "your" drill beforehand out of whatever wood you like...(the dogwood that I use for arrowshafts I prefer)...and splice a tip of your choice for the working end...(see photos).

I find that the outer shell at the base of the cattail is just enough tougher than the inner portion, that it has the tendency to wear faster at the outer edges, leaving our hole looking like an anthill...it won't work this way. To compensate for this I will most times find it necessary to just slightly shave the outside...this takes practice to remove just the right amount...further up the stem I don't find this problem.

This is difficult for me to explain, and probably more difficult

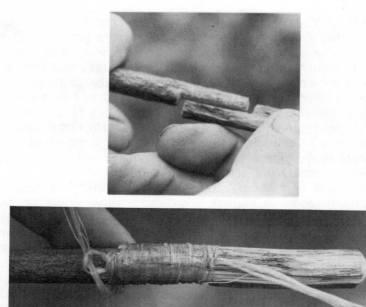

(top) Hand drill spliced to receive a softer tip, here yucca.
(bottom) Splice wrapped with sinew showing how to hide
loose ends...just pull the right hand string and the noose will pull
tight.

Spliced tip ready for service.

for many of you to understand...but before my first sparks
arrived with the hand drill (they still don't come with regularity)
<u>my mind and body became "one" with the drill and fireboard!</u>
You may or may not experience the same... but this has
happened in all cases when I have successfully gotten spark with
the hand drill.

By using a longer drill and SURPERB teamwork, two persons
can make this easier by keeping the drill spinning
constantly...but it takes two working in harmony...one set of
hands picking up at the top when one leaves off at the
bottom.

Another two person variation that I have come up with (I've not heard or seen this anywhere else) which is be far the EASIEST of the hand drill methods that I have worked.
Use a bearing block and have one person apply the downward pressure. The other spins the drill vigorously, instructing the "bearer" how much pressure to apply. The spinner, not having to apply the downward pressure, is not exhausted nearly as easily and the spark can be quickly formed.

CORDAGE

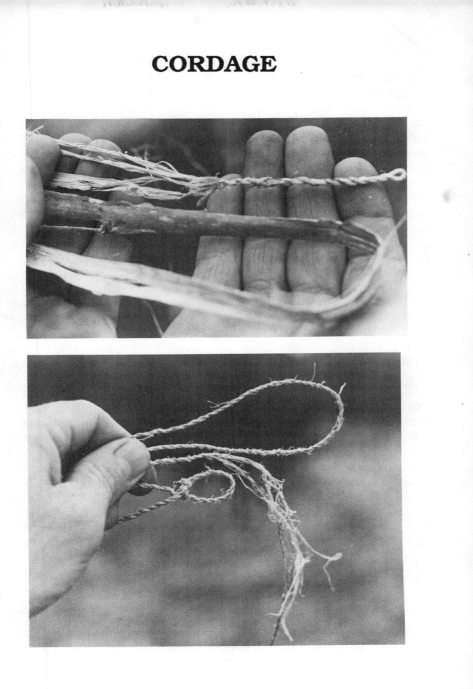

To me, any description of the use of the bow/drill that does not include the making of cordage is incomplete. Such a common thing as a piece of string just isn't always in one's pockets when one may be in need of fire. Especially in a survival situation. And when one most needs this fire (winter, cold and damp), one doesn't really want to (or at least <u>shouldn't</u> want to) tear his or her clothing up to make a string...and even then may not know enough on how to prepare it to keep it from breaking under the stress placed on it by the use of the bow/drill.

This section will teach you how to make usable cordage...cordage that is able to withstand the use of the bow/drill. The ones that I state are usable for this, I have personally used. I will also mention by name others that I've heard or read about but not personally tested. Some you are likely to have with you in the most primitive situation (handkerchief, dog fur, human hair)...others are commonly available afield. For additional sources, once you have soaked up the information contained herein, you can experiment, letting your imagination be your limit.

I am going to attempt to describe this simple craft by words...something not so simply done...and also with the use of photos, a skill that I am more adept at than arranging words.

Take several strands of thread...any kind or size will work. Let's just make these three feet long for this demonstration. Lay them out on a flat surface and use a magic marker (or anything similar) and dye the strands for one third of their length..that's one foot, folks..(you don't have to dye them, remember, this is just to make the process more explainable for me). Pick this bunch of strands up AT THE POINT WHERE THE DYE BEGINS...now, you have hanging from your fingers, two lengths of strands, one being 2 feet long and white...the other 1 foot long and black...Right?...right! You right handers hold them between the thumb and forefinger of your left hand. Let's say that the shorter black strands are now the ones upper most in your grip...begin with these. (my reference to these individual

(preceding page) (top) Hemp cordage still attached to the unprepared strip. (bottom) Sting nettle cordage. This piece "made fire" with the bow/drill.

strands will now be references to either the black or the white...still with me?) Now take these black strands and TWIST THEM TIGHTLY CLOCKWISE...that's to your right, for 1/2" or so. Twist the now twisted black strands COUNTER CLOCKWISE...over the as of yet untwisted whites. Hold them securely. Now twist the whites CLOCKWISE and twist that over the blacks COUNTER CLOCKWISE.

That's it.

The whole secret.

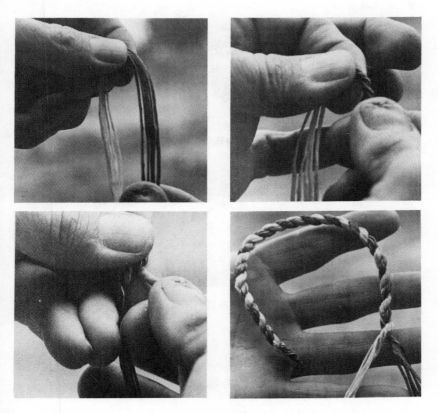

(upper left) Black and white strands hanging from fingers. (upper right) Twisting the blacks tight CLOCKWISE for 'bout half an inch and then (lower left) twisting THAT counter clockwise over the whites and twisting the whites CLOCKWISE. By continuing this simple process you end up with cordage.

Just keep doing this until you are within a few inches of the end of a strand and splice in more to continue for as long as you like. Keep the splices at different intervals on the two sections-- to keep the whole stronger. The twisting CLOCKWISE of the individual strands and twisting them COUNTER CLOCKWISE into one strand is IT. The contrary twisting holds the whole damn thing together. It is a very, very simple concept...until one tries to put it into words.

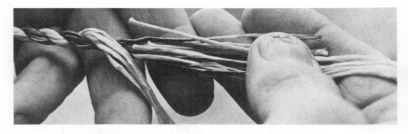

Additional fibers ready to splice in...

Halfway spliced...

and the finished splice.

With this knowledge, your life in the wilds takes on a new dimension . One doesn't have to think for very long before the possible applications start forming. From threads to ropes, the list of uses for cordage is endless...

Cordage materials need not only to be strong enough for the task at hand, but THEY MUST ALSO BE PLIABLE. Though dry grasses would certainly be strong enough for the bow/drill (and also numerous other uses), it's brittleness makes it unusable...it would break immediately just tying a knot.

We'll begin with what you are likely to have with you when thrown into a survival situation. A neckerchief, or something similar, is likely...tear this into strips approximately 1" wide (normal neckerchief is about 18" square)...pick up the first strip as with the fibers (in thirds) and begin the twisting action as before mentioned...when reaching the end of one strip, I tear the last 2" into thirds (also with the new spliced in strand) to help interlock the splice..and on I go. When I reached 3 1/2 ft. with the kerchief I was working, I quit with 5 strips left over. The plus to being able to use this is that in a survival situation one might have access to it, a t-shirt, bandages from a first aid kit...the list of possibilities goes on.

Cordage from neckerchief strips

If you are lucky enough to get lost with a furry critter, so much the better. I worked with the under fur of a dog and found that I had an unlimited supply on hand...and it wasn't all that difficult to get the hang of working with it either, though different than the longer fibers I'm more accustomed to. In a coupla hours, I ended up with a good solid rope about 3 1/2 ft. long. When making fire with it though, I found that it stretched easily and slipped badly on the drill...until I wetted it. Then it worked like a charm. You might also come across the carcass of a furbearer (coon-coyote, etc.) where enough leftover fur might be lying around.

Something that most will have with them is a supply of hair. If things got tight, one could cut his or her own. This does work well. I ended up with a good strong rope in little time (not my own...donated by Margie's Country Image). The hair that I worked with was about 6-8" long, though a bit shorter would work. I also found it much easier to work with if wetted first.

(left) Dog fur and (right) human hair

The list of fibrous plants is long. I'll not be able to cover them all as I don't know them all. Dogbane, which I have read is about the best around, I have never worked with.

Sting nettle, velvetleaf and hemp (marijuana), are three similar, widely distributed and common plants (weeds?). All make a good, strong cordage easily capable of withstanding the stress of the bow/drill. I have tried to work some of these while green with no success. When dried, I take a rounded rock and lightly pound them to break the stalk, and then tear this into

92

strips ('bout thirds). I then begin at the top of the plant and "break" the inner material and then "strip" the outer layer loose. I follow down the plant, breaking and stripping about every inch. (this works better than just "stripping" the outer fibers, which will tear easily.) I end with a rough strip, maybe 2 1/2-3 ft. long. This I will gently roll betwen my fingers or my palms to separate the fibers and to remove the chaff. What you end up with is suitable for cording.

Gently pounding the stalk

Pulling the stalk apart

Breaking the inner stalk and stripping that from the fibers.

The leaf of the yucca gives the strongest cordage of any of the plant fibers that I have worked. It is also easy to work. It has the added advantage of being usable when green or dried. With the yucca leaf, the fibers are in the inside. Take the dried leaf and beat it gently to separate the fibers some. This helps it to soften faster while soaking. Then soak the pounded leaves until they are supple. When like green, or if green, take a rounded knife blade (flint or otherwise) and scrape the outer covering from both sides (the soaking makes this easier with dried leaves). Then work the fibers loose by rubbing back and forth with your fingers. Superb cordage material.

Scraping off the outer covering of the yucca leaf.

94

The spiney yucca plant.

You can come up with additional usable fibers with only a little experimenting. When in the timber or fields, just grab different weeds and grasses as you go along, break them and try to separate the fibers. If they hang together in strips, try using them. Grass will work. It will make a great rough cordage suitable for baskets, mats or insulating liners to winter camps. I haven't tried, but I do believe that the green grass of summer would be capable for the bow/drill, though the dry grases are too brittle for that.

While on the subject of plants, let's not forget the tree barks. The inner barks of many (cedar is my favorite) are fibrous and work superbly as with the fibrous plants. Look around a bit in your area to find what is available.BUT...also, not often thought of, the inner or outer NON-fibrous barks of most trees will work well also (specially for the emergency bow/drill). What I used in my test was the inner bark of the osage orange (I was debarking bow staves). First removing the rough outer bark, I then carefully withdrew thin strips of the next layer. The average

95

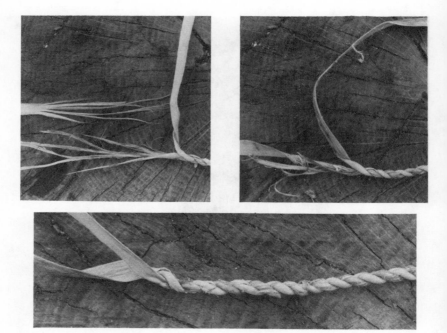

(upper left) Solid piece of bark ready to splice
(upper right) splice halfway worked
(bottom) finished.

length I ended up with was about 3"...a super good length. I cut these down to about 1/4" widths and shaved them until about 1/16th" thick. This individual strip I then used as I would a bunch of strands, twisting away. When I reached the end of a strip, I cut about 2 1/2" of the ends to splice into many thin threads, and continued on. This made ONE OF THE BEST quicky bow/drill strings that I have worked with (besides maybe rawhide). Once dried, it wasn't worth a damn...too stiff and brittle...and you can't cord it when dry...but when wet (green), superb! BUT...when using the bark from any live tree...do so only in an emergency as it does damage the tree (could also kill it). If necessary to use a live tree, take individual strips of bark from several. This helps to ensure the life of the tree. It also would be better for the tree if you stripped the bark from the branches.

Now, let's cover some animal material. Sinew (tendons) supply the strongest cordage available. An animal is loaded with sinew in various lengths, the longest and the easiest to work with being the long strips running down either side of the backbone (silver colored-here lying on top of the meat-running from under the shoulder to the hip). It is most easily removed with a dull knife...so as to help avoid accidently cutting it. Scrape it clean and then lay it out flat to dry. It works easiest if dried first, then broken and separated into threads of the appropriate size...then wetted again before cording. The resulting strong cordage was the most common of the Indian bow strings. The shorter tendons of the legs are also usable...just not as easily since they are shorter and thicker, making them harder to separate and work with.

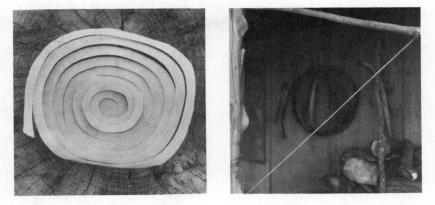

(left) Deer rawhide cut 1/4" wide and
(right) after soaking, doubling and twisting, stretched to dry.

Rawhide is another good cordage material. It is best to use this after drying...primarily because it eliminates stretching (still talking string for the bow/drill). With rawhide, I don't actually "cord" it. Instead I will double it and twist it up pretty tight, stretching it and tying it off at both ends to dry. I find that the doubling, twisting and stretching eliminates the stretching while in use (I use this for bow strings), adds strength and also helps it to somewhat "grip" the drill. I cut the deer rawhide 1/4" wide and it seems to be plenty strong enough. I have shot up to several dozen arrows through 55-60 pound bows that I have made and have yet to have one string break.

I took a squirrel skin and cut this in a circular strip about 1/2" wide, leaving the hair on (as if under a primitive situation), twisted this tight, not doubling it, and made fire the first time (I did have trouble keeping it tied to the bow...with the hair on and the skin green, the knots didn't want to work all that well). The string, as would any green or wet rawhide, stretched badly and took MUCH finger control to keep taking up the slack. Also, after the first fire, I was unable to use the same drill until after it had dried...the moisture from the skin got the drill so wet that it did nothing but slip. Once dried again...no trouble.

Enough for cordage. You've now got enough information to go out, identify certain usable plants (and other materials) and put them to your use. You also have learned enough to be able to search out and experiment to come up with many more. This is not an exact science...just bear in mind the important rules of length and pliability of the material used.

Wild weeds...(left) Velvetleaf and (right) Hemp

98

(The following two pages were originally an addendum to book (now chapter) #5, Primitive Wilderness Cooking Methods.)

A COUPLE TIPS AS SUPPLEMENTS TO MY SECOND BOOK, *"PRIMITIVE FIRE AND CORDAGE"*

<u>Kennie Sherron</u> of Ponca City, Oklahoma sent me the following two fire making ideas that will add greatly to the methods put forth in my book *"Primitive Fire and Cordage"*.

A fire drill, as Kennie describes it, for the Indian who has it all. Made from deer leg bone...is squarish and will never "round". The bone being hollow, it is reinforced at both ends to prevent splitting, here with rawhide. The upper (L) piece is permanent, to fit into the bearing block. The lower, pulled out here, is a replaceable soft tip. When I first got this in the mail, I just kinda put it aside, but carried it along for show and tell. Well, at our last set of demo's we actually ran out of usable drills near the end of the second day...after more than a hundred plus fires...But, we did have some short pieces of yucca..and so gave this a try. I knew that it would work...but was unprepared for how <u>well</u> it worked. The squarish bone spins like a champ in the bow...and the extra weight of the overall drill gave me much better control. And, most importantly, we now had enough fire drill tips for a coupla hundred more fires. I like it!

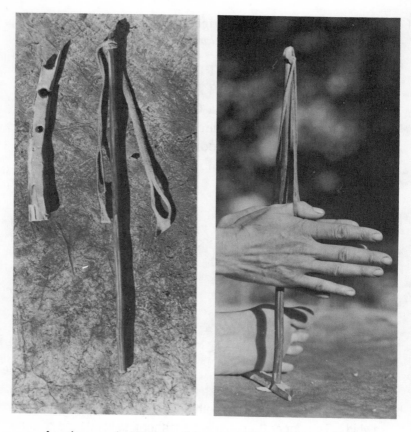

Another, probably more important tip. This for the hand drill...which, under the best of circumstances, is never easy. A piece of cordage, or as illustrated here, a strip of leather (brain tan, of course) with slits cut for the thumbs...tied to the upper end of the drill (and also over in most cases)...The thumbs placed in the slits provides <u>constant</u> downward pressure and you can now constantly spin the drill. Makes this "almost" easy...and greatly increased my successes.

3

Makin' Meat -1

The Primitive Bow and Arrow

INTRODUCTION

Well, here we go again...a third book. What began mostly as a whim with the 'BRAIN TAN BUCKSKIN' book seems to be developing into a series on the skills of primitive living.

My travels around the country since the introduction of my first book has shown a real need and desire for a good instructional set from which even the complete novice to the outdoors would be able to accomplish what at one time for all of us were everyday tasks to our forebears'. MOST literature available on these subjects have given only guidelines...lots of philosophy and just about enough information to get one interested...and into trouble. I know that my personal learning of these skills was not easy. I followed (or tried to) what little information that I could find in print. It just wasn't available. By mainly trial and error I got to the point that I felt confident enough to go "Naked into the Wilderness".

I've spent the last coupla years traveling the country, mostly to the mountain man rendezvous', but also to various museums, private groups, National Historic Sites and festivals, teaching some of these primitive skills...and it seems that no matter where I'm at, there just ain't enough daylight hours. There is a real hunger for these skills...especially when they are taken out of the realm of magicians and made simple enough to understand so that just about any person of average intelligence and dexterity can accomplish them.

There is no big secret to mastering any of this. It's all just basic physics. When once learned, you will say, "well, hell yes...why didn't I think of that"! Some...no...much of it is time consuming...especially in this day of "instant" everything. But I am finding that many, many people are just pretty sick and tired of all the hustle. This consumer oriented/industrialized society that we belong to has made most of its inhabitants dependant upon others for even the simplest of needs.

These skills, once learned, BECAUSE OF THEIR SIMPLICITY, will be with you from now on 'til forever...and that's a mighty long time. They need not be applied or practiced every day to stay fresh with-in your mind. And the comfort that comes from just <u>knowing</u> them will give you the freedom of self to know that you are self-sufficient to the extreme. Though most will never apply them as such, the knowledge that you need depend on no other man to survive is mighty re-assuring.

My first book, 'BRAIN TAN BUCKSKIN' , was written with no thought of writing more in the future. But because of it's success, and many requests, the second, 'PRIMITIVE FIRE AND CORDAGE', was born...and also the thoughts of a complete series: to take the individual, regardless of his or her outdoor experience, step by step through the skills necessary to take to the wilderness and not only survive, but to live comfortably.

I have found that many people who know of and talk/write/teach some of these skills, take the student through to a finished primitive product or skill <u>from today backwards</u>...using today's technology to a primitive end. I was guilty of it myself in the first of my books...using nylon cords, steel blades, etc. I've found that the reason that I (and others of my ilk) are so rounded in our outdoor education is that we taught ourselves these skills with from nothing — forward...how to go "Naked into the Wilderness" (which is to be the title of the finished series) and to live.

An example: the primitive arrow. To go from nothing, forward, one first needs some insight as to the type of wood to use...a knowledge, however simple, of working with stone tools to peel and smooth the shaft...how to make fire so that the shaft can be heated and straightened...a knowledge of cordage so as to apply the fletching and point. A step up from the most primitive of arrows requires the skills to work flint or bone to make a more serviceable point...and to apply them well, the knowledge of boiling down hide scrapings, and other animal parts, to make glue...without the advantage of a pot. That's a lot of different skills needed for just one arrow.

I plan on ending up with six or eight booklets in this series, each taking the reader a step back (or forward) in his or her education. Any one of the books will be able to be taken by itself to master a particular skill or interest...but one will always overlap to the others for the "complete" knowledge. The BRAIN TAN book also includes a chapter on sinew...which I did not delve into in the book on FIRE AND CORDAGE...and from now on I will only make reference to these as the need for them arises.

This book, "MAKIN' MEAT -1", was, in it's original concept, going to be but one book to cover some of the various methods of gathering subsistence in the wilderness, beginning with the bow and arrow...but...well, I just ran outta room. I plan to keep the price of all these books at $3.00. By the time that I had finished the instructions on the primitive bow and arrow, I found that I had filled the allocated pages for one book. Therefore the two (or maybe more) books on "Makin' Meat". Book 2, which will follow as soon as I get this one paid for, will go into the use of snares/deadfalls/marine life/insects, etc. to obtain subsistance in the wilds.

I don't pretend to have enough knowledge of edible plants to even mention them. It is a skill that in itself requires years, if not a lifetime, of learning. Certainly, I have learned a little along these lines in the acquiring of other knowledge, but I can spend six weeks, or less, with an individual and teach him or her how to live WELL in the out of doors, including how to obtain subsistence to live. In that period of time I wouldn't even have my foot in the door when it comes to edible plants. To me, this knowledge would be nice to know...someday.

Now, the methods that I describe here are MINE. They work for me. what I describe as cardinal rules, not to be ventured from, are broken all the time by a bowmaker friend of mine. And his bows work great. So what I describe is not the ONLY way...but it do work for me!!! And what I describe as happening to the wood at various stages may not be in actuality. But if you approach the project thinking the way that I describe it, the finished product will be workable...and that's what counts.

We'll be using hand tools here. Not the primitive tools that will be required in a strictly primitive situation, but modern "white man tools". The using of stone and bone for tools will be covered in a later book.

I'll also be throwing in ideas and tips that I've picked from various sources. What I put forth does work...but as I stress, It's not the only way. In fact, through the entire series, I'll be showing you how to accomplish the task at hand...but will also keep the door open so that you may use your own ideas to come up with other, and quite possibly better, ways to accomplish the same end.

Well, enough ramblin' lets get to work.

December 1987

This book was, as far as I know, only the second one published in recent years that gave specific instructions on how one could go about turning a tree into a working bow --- specifically a "how to". Since then there probably have been a dozen books written on the same subject ... people who have some "secret ingredient" to offer the reader. Most are just a re-hashing of the same principles. Some better written than others. *Some* of what is out there is just plain trash. A market exists and there is always someone to find a way to make a quick buck. A lot of material exists for one to look thru ... especially if one don't know just what he/she is looking for. One point about *this* book that I do want to stress is cost. There are books out there costing up to and more than five times as much as this one ... and offering nothing more. The $3..00 price tag that I began working with seven years ago is still in effect. *It just don't cost that much to put a book together*. A lot of people are making one hell of a lot of money. Believe me, you just won't learn any more about the simple art of making a bow in over 90% of what's available, regardless of price, than you will with this one.

At the appearance of one of the better books, I read thru this one a coupla times to see how it compared ... should I revise it? ... or what. After each re-reading I was satisfied that this book accomplished its purpose ... to teach one **how** to make a bow. It don't tell how to make it pretty, it tells how to make one that will shoot an arrow satisfactorily

Since first writing this book almost five years ago, I sure have learned a lot about the makings and workings of bows ... the why's, so to speak. This book in its original form is good enough to leave as is. It works! It tells how. This insert is to explain some of the why's.

ANATOMY OF A BOW

Simply put, a bow is a stick with a string tied at each end that will propel an arrow. In order to understand how to successfully make this stick bend time and again to its full potential, we need a quick lesson in physics. So, pay close attention ... this is important.

• Any piece of wood of equal dimensions from end to end will bend at the middle when force is applied. To counteract this, we remove wood from the limbs of our bow ... more from nearer the tips than from closer to the grip.

• In the removal of wood in shaping and tillering of the bow, an equation is of importance. If half of the wood is removed in the *width* of the bow, the strength is halved. If half of the wood is removed in the *thickness* of the bow, the strength is decreased by **8 times!** What this is saying is that the bow will be more effective if it is narrower and thicker, especially at the tips. (This is explained shortly.)

• The outside of the bend (back of the bow) will be trying to tear apart

tension). The inside (belly) will be compressing.

• *Most woods are stronger under tension than under compression.* The fibers of most woods will fail first under compression ... almost immediately followed by the tearing apart of the back leaving one with the false impression that the back failed first.

• Tillering, equal bending of the limbs, is critical. If a portion of the limb is not bending,, somewhere else is bending too much - failure will result.

• Somewhere towards the center (between back & belly) of this piece of wood is a neutral plane where no forces are in effect (that we need be aware of here). From this neutral plane outward in each direction, all of, or 100%, of the forces of tension and compression are being exerted. Simple, yes. *But* ... the closer to the neutral plane, the less force exerted. So, how this effects us is that the nearer the outside (either side), the furthest from the neutral plane, is where most of the percentage of tension and compression are occurring. So, a higher percentage of tension & compression is taking place in a smaller percentage of the wood. 50% of these forces are happening in the outer 10% of the wood. What that is telling us is that a flat outer surface will make a stronger bow because then this higher percentage of forces is spread over a wider surface. The backs of bows, we don't have that much control over ... we need follow the growth ring of the tree. The smaller the tree or limb, the rounder the outer surface, the more tension exerted in a smaller area. But, the belly we do have control over. That we can make flat. And since the majority of woods fail first under compression, this works to our advantage.

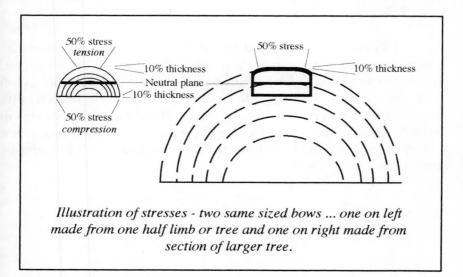

Illustration of stresses - two same sized bows ... one on left made from one half limb or tree and one on right made from section of larger tree.

• Mass of the wood - the actual bow itself - slows down the working action or response and so directly affects the performance of the arrow. This most noticeable towards the tips of the bow. So, the less mass (wood/weight for a particular weight bow, the better the performance.

• Each piece of wood has its ideal width to thickness ratio ... general speaking the harder the wood, the narrower this is. The narrower that you ca make your bow, the more effective it will be because it will contain its least mass. Less mass means faster performance. *BUT*...

• What we are after in our chosen piece of wood is the ratio whereby the bow can be bent to its fullest extent and to have this wood not fail under either tension or compression (all woods will fail if pulled too far). Lets assu our wood is stronger under tension and that we have an unviolated back ... a we need concern ourselves with now is compression. ALL woods will fail under compression to some extent. Our ideal bow will fail only slightly noti able. Assuming that we are working with a straight bow, we will end with o slight string follow when the bow has been broken in. This is where we wan get our particular bow. Each wood will be different ... each round from the same tree will be somewhat different. There is no set formula. A hard wood such as osage orange will reach this stage being thicker and narrower than a comparable piece of, lets say, hickory, another hard wood.

• A straight bow made to this perfection, the same length and weigh lets say 48" and 55#, the specific gravity (weight) being about equal, the narrower, thicker bow will shoot farther and faster because it will contain le mass (2:1 compared to 8:1).

This knowledge hasn't just appeared to me in dreams but has come from many sources ... some even the aforementioned books. But the largest contributors to making my mind think bows have been *Jeff Schmidt*, a prof sor of physics whose workings with the Asian composite bow (a book of its own) has enlightened me to the physics involved and *Tim Baker* who has d the most extensive research and testing of the primitive bow of anyone I kno To both of these fine folks, my thanx for their complete unselfish sharing of information.

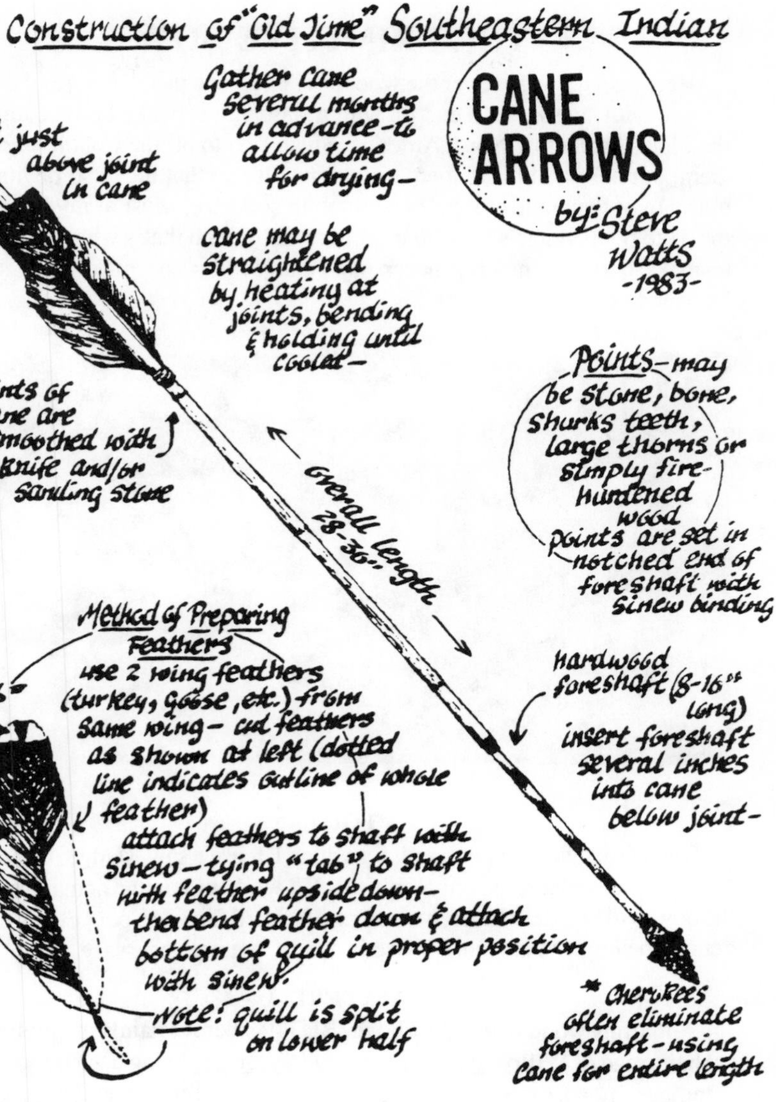

Construction of "Old Time" Southeastern Indian

CANE ARROWS
by: Steve Watts
-1983-

Gather cane several months in advance—to allow time for drying—

cane may be straightened by heating at joints, bending & holding until cooled—

"V" cut just above joint in cane

joints of cane are smoothed with knife and/or sanding stone

Overall length 28-36"

Points—may be stone, bone, sharks teeth, large thorns or simply fire-hardened wood

points are set in notched end of foreshaft with sinew binding

hardwood foreshaft (8-16" long)

insert foreshaft several inches into cane below joint—

Method of Preparing Feathers

use 2 wing feathers (turkey, goose, etc.) from same wing— cut feathers as shown at left (dotted line indicates outline of whole feather)

"tab"

attach feathers to shaft with sinew—tying "tab" to shaft with feather upside down—then bend feather down & attach bottom of quill in proper position with sinew.

Note! quill is split on lower half

* Cherokees often eliminate foreshaft—using cane for entire length

A FLYER BORROWED FROM STEVE WATTS OF GASTONIA, N.C. ON CONSTRUCTION OF OLD TIME S.E. CANE ARROWS

THE PRIMITIVE BOW

Here I am going to cover the wooden self (all one piece) bow, and the same backed with sinew. We'll end up with a short sinew backed bow common to the Plains Indians of North America. Since I go to all the trouble of making them, not only do I make them usable but also so that they can be hung in a museum or the home of the discriminating collector. Most of my bows are in the 55 to 60 lb. range with a 20 to 22 inch arrow, and that's what we are going to make here. By making necessary changes you can make your's either heavier or lighter.

TOOLS

Once the staves are prepared, for which I'll use a saw, sledge, heavy knife of sorts and wedges, the only tools that I'll work with in the actual making of the bow will be a drawknife, a wood rasp/bastard file and a pocket knife. Can't get much simpler than that. A vise is handy, but not necessary.

MATERIAL

About any wood will make a bow...BUT!!! There certainly are preferences. I have read of <u>Willow, Cottonwood</u> and <u>Sycamore</u> being used by some early Indians...not of preference, but because of availability. <u>Osage Orange</u>, I know from experience, makes one of the best bows...<u>Yew</u>, a close competitor. <u>White Oak</u> makes a real fine bow, and it's a bit easier to work than Osage. The bow that we will make here will be <u>Hickory</u>...not one of the better woods (just not as much snap as the others) , but one that I highly recommend for the beginning bowmaker. It's a real forgiving wood and almost impossible to break. I have had Osage bows break on me when they shouldn't have...even after having been backed with sinew and shot several times. And

I also just recently had a White Oak bow that had been backed with sinew three times and shot for several months, break for no apparent reason. Lots of frustration when a bow breaks...so I think that one should work with more of a sure thing for the first. The same steps illustrated here will apply with all woods.

The list of preferred woods really isn't very long. <u>Ash, Black Locust, Lemonwood</u> and <u>Mulberry</u> are some of the others. But, what was available is what was used in days gone by.

Generally the softer, more brittle woods (Yew / Cedar) were made into wide, flat bows and the harder/denser woods (Osage/White Oak) made into narrow thick bows.

FINDING THE STAVE

The perfect stave would be straight, knot free, resilient and would spring back to it's original shape when unstrung, not staying bent (following the string)...and it would be snappy...kinda like spring steel. A lot to ask for in one piece of wood.

I cut most all of my staves green, in the dead of winter when the sap is down (excess moisture takes longer to cure and leads to more checking / cracking). Occasionally I find a dead limb/tree that is ready to work in one of the hard/dense woods...but not often.

I want the stave as straight as possible, though they can be heated and straightened to a great extent later on.

I watch for knots. Best if there are none...but I've made several good bows by working around them...which will be explained later.

I take limbs or trunks of any size 2 1/2 inches or thicker. You could get by with smaller, but I like the extra freedom of material to work with. With the smaller size, I only try to get one good stave from the round...it's not all that easy to split the smaller staves exactly in half. The larger pieces I can get several staves from by careful splitting.

CURING

I've read and heard of as many ways to cure out a stave as I have heard of making bows. Some bury them in their gardens from six months to six years...some cover the ends, or the entire log, with wax...to allow the log to cure slowly and minimize warpage and cracking...and on, and on. I have also heard not to use kiln dried wood.

Now, some of my own thinking. Green wood won't work...it's resilient enough to take the stress of bending, but too slow in response to cast an arrow. The drier the wood, the faster (snappier)...but too dry makes the wood too brittle...leading to breakage (therefore not kiln dried wood). So we need something in between.

The heavier dense woods need longer to cure then the looser grained woods. The densest and heaviest will include Osage and White Oak. The other extreme to include Yew and Cedar...with most somewhere in between...as is our model, hickory.

I take ALL my staves and I first debark them and right away I split them into the size stave that works out best. When debarking, much care needs to be taken so as to NOT cut through the outer growth ring. In fact, it is wise to leave just the slightest bit of inner bark on the stave to insure this. I then split to separate the heart (inside) wood from the sap (outside) wood. The heart is denser and therefore dries at a different rate than the sap...which is a major cause of warpage and cracking. Sometimes I am able to save for usable staves both the heart and sap woods...but more often I must choose.

With hickory I find that the sapwood is thicker than the heart, so I usually save the sap. With White Oak I save the heart...the same with Osage (I know of one bowmaker who leaves the sap of Osage on the heart, which is only about 1/4 inch thick or less, and it acts as a sort of a lamination allowing for more flexibility).

When splitting out the staves, with the bark off I can more easily see the knots and how the grain of wood flows. This dictates just where to split. Knot free if possible...knots in the center of the wood are pretty much negligent, as also are knots in the grip portion. Knots close to the edge should be pretty much avoided. More on that later. Let the piece of wood that you are working with dictate the working of the bow.

If there is an average to the size of my staves, they would be about 1 1/2 inch thick by about 2 1/2 inches wide by however long. All either wood of the heart

or the sap. These I will hang in a covered area out of doors for about six to eight weeks when I'll take them in by the fire for about another two to four weeks. Then, I make bows from them.

I have successfully made bows from Osage, White Oak and Hickory in as short a time from cutting as this.

110

MAKING THE BOW

So let's now take hold of our cured stave. Plan to spend some time with it. Feel it. Look it over very carefully. Study it.

The rules to remember now are (1) to work with the grain. Follow the grain of the wood from one end of the stave to the other...(2) NEVER cut through the outside (back...the side away from the shooter) growth ring. This I stress as a must, (though I know of at least one other who always breaks this rule.) If once, the ring is cut through, remove the entire ring down to the next. Otherwise, this is where the bow is most liable to break. (3) Keep the knots to the inside of the bow. When a knot cannot be avoided at the edge, DO NOT CUT THROUGH THE NATURAL FLOW OF THE FIBERS AROUND IT. Leave a bit of a bump there, it will just add character to the finished product. Cutting through the fibers will only weaken the limb at this point (a good friend of mine, a bowmaker, say's just the opposite).

When studied long enough, the bow will appear to you with-in the stave. Follow the line of longitude grain and begin placing knots where they will do no harm...eliminate all that you can. Is a narrow, thick bow called for or one that is wide and flat? Every piece of wood speaks differently...no two bows will be exactly alike. Take a pencil and draw an outline of your bow...making the center grip a bit longer than your hand is wide. When you have searched it out for the best possible section for a bow...looked it over from all sides and drawn your outline, then you are ready to pick up the drawknife.

111

It is easiest to work with the aid of a vise...though I have free handed some and have also come up with a coupla contraptions to work in the wild. I will normally work first the sides of the stave to the outline that I have drawn, though each piece will be different. I try to do this first because when I begin working on the thickness of the limbs, I can be more accurate in judging the weight of the bow and feeling the bend of the limbs if it is almost to its proper width. At this point keep the entire bow just slightly oversized so that when heated to bend, if inadvertently scorched, there will be room to remove some. Once the width is about within 1/8th of an inch or so, begin working on the belly. Remember, no more is to be removed from the back!

I'll begin shaping with the grip. Just whatever feels good to you. It's best to keep it thicker here then in the limbs so there will be no bend, which will cause it to kick...but careful study of old bows shows that for the most part Indians didn't worry much about this. The limbs should taper gradually from the grip to the tips. Work it slowly. Remember, once it's removed, it can't be put back. Once I get to with-in about 1/4th inch of the final size, I'll put aside the drawknife and take up a wood rasp, as occasionally the knife will take a bit larger bite than I want. As the limb gets with-in bending range, slow down and feel your way carefully. Try to remove from the entire limb at the same time. When it begins to show bendability, back away from the grip and work only the rest of the limb...and so on until you get to the tip. At this stage, the limb should bend pretty evenly between the nock and the grip...but still be much too strong to even consider stringing. When one limb is about where you want it, repeat with the other. The 2nd limb will be more difficult as you will be trying to match the first. Just work slowly...a little at a time. Keep a constant check on your progress by bending the bow over your knee. You don't need to be exact. Just eyeball it. This isn't the finished size yet.

Note deep cut caused by careless use of the drawknife...it's best to go slow and easy, leaving a lot for the wood rasp.

Now, before you get too confused as to some of the terminology that I'm using here, I'll include a short glossary of terms that I use.

The BACK of the bow is the side that is away from you when the bow is strung....the BELLY, the side facing you. The GRIP is the center of the bow which you grip when shooting. The LIMB is the section on either side of the grip running to the TIP. The EARS, if a bow has them, are the four to six inches at the tip that are bent back away from the belly, in effect shortening the bow. NOTCHES are the depressions cut near the tips to hold the string.

Study CAREFULLY the series of photographs on the next two pages....they will take you from the raw stave through to the bow prepared for the first heating session.

114

HEATING AND BENDING

Once you have the limbs bending pretty uniformly, it is time to do any bending of the bow that you may need or want to. It's not very often that I begin with a perfectly straight stave as I usually save my best to sell, making my bows from the harder to work pieces. Every bow that I have worked has NEEDED straightening, which will be the first step. Once I get a straight bow, then I can decide as to how I want to bend it to shape. Sometimes, I leave it straight. Most often I will reflex (bend in the opposite direction) the bow because all woods will initially follow the string somewhat...especially Hickory. I often will bend the ears back also, but the purpose of this is to shorten the bow and make it faster, and we are here already working with a short bow.

I once put ears on a beautiful Osage bow that I made...a nice 42 inch long bow. I afterwards had to thin the ears to allow them to bend because all the bend was forced into one small area of the limbs. I had already sinewed the back and so was unable to heat and straighten. Ears do, though, make for a real nice looking bow.

The actual heating of the wood is done slowly. It can be done over an open fire, hot coals, the flame of a gas range or even an electric range. The idea is to heat the fibers of the wood COMPLETELY THROUGH. I apply grease (poly-unsaturated bear grease - Crisco) liberally on the spot that I am heating. I have in the past just steamed it but it takes much too long. I have heard of others who use water in lieu of grease. Some even boil it.. To my way of thinking, the grease/water serves two purposes. (1) To help protect the wood from scorching (which will make the wood brittle and worthless) and (2) to allow moisture (in the form of steam?) to penetrate through the fibers of the wood. Whether that is so or not, that is the way I look at it. Whatever, it do work. When the fibers are heated completely through, the wood will bend as easily as it does when green...BUT...if kept in it's new position until it cools,

116

it will stay there. You must be careful and not over-do it. It is easy enough to take it too far and tear or break the fibers...you will have to feel this as you go. Heat, bend a little, reheat, bend some more. When it breaks, you've gone too far. I've never had a piece break while doing this. Some bowmakers make a jig and place the bow into it until it is completely cooled. I just hold it in position for about 30 to 45 seconds and it seems to stay pretty close to where I want it. Keep the piece MOVING CONSTANTLY over the fire, never letting it stay exposed to the heat at any one spot for too long...which will lead to scorching (the purpose of leaving the bow oversize til now was to give something extra to remove in the event that it was scorched a little). If I'm wanting to bend only a small area, I will heat an area about three to four inches long. If the bend or twist - (yes, twists can be eliminated if they are not too bad) is spread over a longer area, heat it all. In about three to five minutes, a small area should be hot enough to bend...depending on the thickness. I cannot over impress on you the importance of not scorching. Go slow.

Note scorch - reason for leaving oversize - brittle protion will be removed

Now, another important point. Heat and bend an area on one limb. If there is a spot that you can also work on the other limb which will not interfere with the spot that you've just bent (straightened), do it also. Then lay it aside until it has a chance to COMPLETELY cool. If you try to do too much at one time, areas that have already been worked, but are still warm with-in, can easily be re-bent. This is not something to be done at one sitting. Some of my bows take several days to get to where I'm satisfied with them...don't get over anxious.

I will take the bow to straight first...(unless a natural bend can be used advantageously in the finished shape of the bow) ...then do whatever shaping that I deem necessary. I have read and heard from several sources that if one part of a bow is heated, you should do the same spot to the other limb. I don't bother about that.

117

Bow taken to straight

FINAL WORKING

When all of the heating/straightening/bending is done, now is the time to get down to the nitty-gritty of finishing your project.

With rasp in hand, approach the bow cautiously...actually from now on the bastard file will get the most use. Carefully, we are going to remove wood to the final size..slowly, so as not to overdo it. Remember, it can't be put back.

Usually, but not always, the grip will need no further work. If, though, it was left oversize, for the purpose of straightening or whatever, start here. Work it down til you have what you want. Don't just jump in and start filing away though, look it over form all sides and remove so that things stay uniform. From there, one limb at a time, begin workin out to the tips. BELLY AND SIDES OF THE BOW ONLY. NOTHING IS TO BE TOUCHED ON THE BACK OF THE BOW!!! Work easy, bending it every so often over the knee to feel it's strength. When one limb feels and looks about right, go to the other. Now we are going to be watching both limbs as we bend...we want the bend to be the same (tillering the bow). 90% of my bows are done completely by eyesight and feel. I'm pretty certain from the examples that I've seen that the Indian had no calipers or tillering machine...do here what you want.

The last coupla paragraphs won't take but a minute to read...but in doing, expect to spend the better part of a day to do it right.

Remember when finishing..we are going to remove any scorched areas (except from the back. If you have scorched here, it'd be best to start

118

over)...they are brittle and will break easily...weak spots. We are going to be tillering the limbs but WE ARE NOT GONNA TOUCH THE BACK OF THE BOW!!!

Carefully - removing just a little at a time

When satisfied, now is the time to cut our nocks for the string and to string the bow. Here, any <u>strong</u> cord will suffice. (Strings will be covered pretty shortly.) The cuts for notches can be done about any way that you like, they need only be near the tip of the limbs...suitable to hold the string. Many old bows had no nock at all... only a build-up of sinew to prevent the string from sliding down the shaft. The photo's show the way that I do mine. Old bows were done in many ways...but the most common method of the Plains Indians was to put two nocks on the lower end of the bow and one on the upper. This is what I normally do.

The bow, before final heating and finishing draws 50 lb. at 15 1/4 inches.

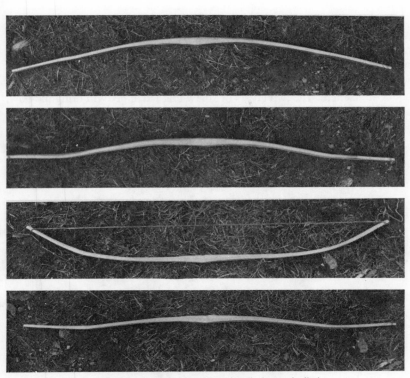

Series showing steps in bending. In all photos belly is up.
#1-- Both limbs reflexed at grip
#2 - Towards the tips curved back in
#3 - Bow now strung, tested 45 lbs. at 22" draw
#4 - Showing how bow somewhat followed string from just one time stringing

Final tillering can't be done until we've strung the bow. If we have watched what we are doing up til now, the limbs should be pretty close. The first thing that I do after stringing for the first time, is to pull easily to "feel" how it pulls. With the short bows that I make, I use an arrow pretty close to one half the bows' length, usually 20 to 22 inches. I'll use a premeasured stick or an arrow to check this. The short bows "stack up" pretty fast (by stacking up I mean that they suddenly get harder and harder to pull). Pull gently at first. Now is a good (bad) time to break it...Feel it out. If the wood does suddenly feel that it won't give any more, listen to it. Remove some more wood FROM THE BELLY to limber it.

121

With most of my bows, I like to end at this stage with about a 45 lb pull at what I have decided the arrow length to be. This I measure by pulling from a scale. Whatever the scale reads at the full draw length is what I call the bow weight. I don't know how the "big boys" do it. Bows can be made to pull at whatever weight you desire, but as I back all of mine with sinew I keep it at about 45 lbs here. The two layers of sinew that I'll apply will bring the bow, after final tillering, to 55 to 60 lbs.

Checking bendability of bow constantly as we go

At this point we have a finished, shootable self bow of about 45 lbs draw weight with a 22 inch arrow.

If we were to keep it here and not go on to sinew it, it would call for some sort of sealing to protect it from the elements. In the old days, grease was liberally applied...and re-applied...and even some more, for the purpose of keeping the bow limber. Most times, the bow would be heated somewhat and then the grease (and maybe brains) applied.

My thinking again...If kept in the moisture, unprotected, for long, the wood would soak up moisture and become weaker and subject to rot. If kept unprotected in a low humidity area, It would dry to the point that it would become too brittle and therefore subject to breakage.

Whatever, you can stop here if you want. I never do. Next for me is to......

122

BACK THE BOW WITH SINEW

Remember what I said earlier about the ideal bowstave having the quality of springing back to it's original shape when unstrung? Well, many woods don't possess that quality. In fact, the Hickory bow that has just been made is one of the worst for "following the string". It wouldn't be too very long before the bow would be bent almost to the point that it would require no additional bending to string it.

Applying of sinew to the back of the bow will help greatly in reducing this tendency. It will also add strength, power and "snap" to the bow (Hickory is a very sluggish wood). And it will also add greatly to the elasticity of the bow. On some bows where I haven't reached the desired draw length and haven't wanted to shave away any more wood, I've gone ahead and sinewed and then have been able to increase the draw. The application of sinew really does a lot for the wood.

Read through this section thoroughly and understand it completely before proceeding. This step is kinda complicated to describe, even with the help of photo's, but the actual process of sinewing is really much easier than describing it. When you understand just what you are doing...why you are doing it...with what you are doing it...and how to do it...doing it will be a piece of cake. Remember also that here we are working in the kitchen. It's really not all that much more difficult to do in the wilds...just much more time consuming.

Three strips of deer sinew - two partially separated

123

Sinew...is tendon. Available from all animals...including us. The two most useful pieces are taken either from the legs, or preferably, from either side of the backbone. The sinew from the legs works, but is shorter by far than the loin sinew and for this reason, I don't use it...although I do keep some on hand. The much longer strips, one lying on either side of the backbone, is a lot more pleasurable working with and is easily enough removed from the carcass of any large animal (Removal from the animal and preparation of threads is described fully in my book "BRAIN TAN BUCKSKIN').

Leg sinew must be pounded thoroughly and then separated into threads. The loin sinew, if cleaned properly, has only to be roughened between the fingers first (we're talking about two or three minutes work here) and then separated into threads. I try to keep the threads all about a good 1/8th inch thick. I have found that three average loin strips of deer sinew will allow me to apply two coats to the bow and have enough left over for the bow string. The entire process of preparing the threads will take not much more than an hour.

To prepare the bow, it must be washed thoroughly. All grease and oils must be removed for the glue and sinew to adhere...and that includes the oils from your hands. Some wash their bows with lye. I did on two bows...didn't like working with the caustic stuff...and went back to my method of a good scrubbing, a toothbrush works well, Ivory dish soap and lots of HOT, HOT, HOT water...rinsed very thoroughly. Wash also the belly of the bow for a coupla inches down from the tips at either end. The bow can be sinewed either damp or dry, I have found no difference. Now, don't touch the back of the bow with your hands again until you are applying the glue.

Also...the nap of the wood on the back of the bow must be raised so that the glue has something to adhere to. This can be accomplished with either a file or a hacksaw blade...work gently so as to only raise the nap. Don't go so deep that you cut through the growth ring. This can be done either before or after the washing.

GLUE

Here I am going to break one of my rules and make a statement that I haven't personally tested to see if true...but is common consensus among all bow-makers with whom I've spoken. "Sinew is protein. The only glue that can successfully be used with it is another pure protein...hide glue". It makes sense to me and that is all that I've ever used with sinew. And it does work. I haven't tried any of the other commercial glues available...sinew is not all that easy to come by and I don't want to take the chance on ruining any. Hide glue I have always had access to...or have taken the time to make it.

Hide glue can be made, as the name implies, from hide. Get a pot of water boiling and add (or add and then get to boiling) hide scrapings, pieces of rawhide, scraps of sinew, pieces of horn or hoof...and I have even heard of boiling the penis (which I haven't tried). It will take a lot of boiling...or simmering. The smaller the pieces, the quicker. Eventually (several hours...sometimes several, several hours) it will get to about the consistency of molasses. Remove whatever oils that are on the surface (I have heard tell that this is pure neatsfoot oil...don't know), but what is left is hide glue. It can be used as is or dried, til hard as a rock, and pulverized. Then mixed with boiling water for later use. Glue sticks can also be made from this, real handy for small jobs. Just keep globbing it on the end of a stick til you've got a nice ball of it...remember, though, that it will shrink considerably as it dries.

It can also be bought. Making it can be a real pain and time consuming (being hypocritical now ain't I) so anymore I do buy most of what I use. It's available either granulated as I just described, or in a liquid form. I made a coupla bows years ago using this liquid stuff. It worked, but took forever to cure out and always seemed tacky. I read in D.C. Waldorf's book (THE ART OF MAKING PRIMITIVE BOWS AND ARROWS), that this was due to an additive and that it could be counteracted by adding vinegar. I tried that once but still didn't like working with it all that much. It's not all that easy to find the granulated glue at times though. You might try art supply stores and especially places that work with stained glass. The only source that I know of at present that keeps a supply on hand at most times is:

Ray's Beaver Bag
727 Las Vegas Blvd. S.
Las Vegas, Nevada 89101

Figure on paying about $10.00 a pound. That sounds like a lot but a pound of glue will make three, four or even more bows with plenty of leftovers for arrows and other crafty things.

Now that we have all of the components together...sinew threads, hide glue and the prepared bow...lets get going. I'll explain my set-up and you can devise whatever will work best for you.

I work with two dish pans. One holds the bow for easy workability, back side up. In it I put about 1 1/2 to 2 inches of COLD water to soak the sinew

125

threads. Begin by soaking about one third (one loin strip) of your threads (assuming that you have used three deer loin sinews) or whatever. I like to soak them for several minutes...they become elastic when soaked and shrink as they dry, there-by adding their strength to the bow. HOT water will cook them...WARM will cause them to curl.

As these are soaking, add a coupla cups of boiling water to a handful or so of the hide glue crystals in a third smaller pan. This is variable...you don't want it too watery but also not too thick...about like a thin syrup. With a lot of stirring, the glue will eventually dissolve in the boiling hot water.

The working temp of the glue should be about 115 to 120 degrees F. Just warm to the touch. The glue will set up FAST at about 85 to 90 degrees.

I find working at a room temp of about 85 degrees just about right. I prefer it to set up kinda quick. The hotter the room, the slower the set up time. Therefore you might find it easier working during the cold of winter when the room temp. is easier to control than on a 75 to 80 degree day.

Place the pan holding the now liquid glue into a third, somewhat larger pan containing HOT water...like a double boiler...to keep it at a good working temp. Though the hands, bow and glue would stand hotter temps, the sinew won't. So keep it just warm enough.

Put newspapers under all...things are about to get real sticky.

First...apply one or two coats of glue to the back of the bow...allow to become tacky.

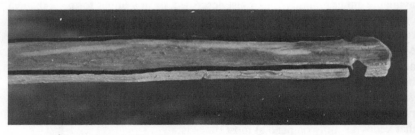

End of bow coated with glue and one thread "ridging" the outside- I inked in ridge thread to make it show.

The purpose now is to cover the entire back of the bow with an even layer of sinew threads...one thread deep. Try to avoid having bunches of threads meeting at the same "joint" (butt to butt)...as in laying brick or stone...overlap the threads. One by one, take the threads from the water...squeeze the excess moisture out of them between thumb and fore finger...Dip it into the glue...squeeze out the excess between thumb and fore finger...then dip it into the glue once again and again squeeze out the excess (if the thread is left to

126

soak in the glue, it will begin to cook/curl)...now lay the thread onto the back of the bow. I begin by placing the first threads along the very edge of the bow...from one end to the other, going through whatever nock there may be and on to the other side...if no nock, as in my one nock end, then go over the tip and down the other side for a coupla inches.

When applying this first layer of sinew, I prefer to make this "ridge" on either side of the bow as it serves as a guideline, making it easier for me to fill the space in between evenly. I know of others who count each thread to make certain that an equal number is placed on each limb. For this first layer, it's not necessary. The entire back needs to be covered for the best response. If the bow is tillered pretty close, the limbs should be about equal widths anyhow. The only way that you might run into trouble is by placing threads of different sizes on the opposite limbs. If the threads are pretty close, you'll have no troubles.

You'll note that I said to run the threads over the tips and down the other sides a coupla inches. If there is to be more than one coating, this wouldn't be a necessity at this time (though I do all mine). But with the final layer, the threads are carried over and then held in place by wrapping with a sinew thread to keep the ends from pulling loose.

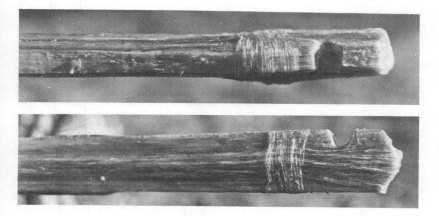

I invariably apply two coats of sinew to my bows. After the first is in place, I take a 15 to 20 minute break to allow the first to somewhat set up. Also it should be about time to begin soaking more threads, if you haven't had to do so by now. For the 2nd layer, I usually don't use quite as much sinew as I did in the first...unless I'm really trying to add power to a particular bow.

For this layer...I count the threads. 12 on one limb...12 on the other. These threads are all placed down the center of the bow, not as an even layer as with the first. The threads will spread out as you apply them and the finished appearance will be slightly rounded. From one to three dozen threads to each limb should do the trick here. Remember not to butt the ends, but to overlap...and also to carry the threads over the tips and down the other side a bit.

You will find that you will have to replace the HOT water in your tray once or twice to keep the glue at it's proper temp.

You will also find "globs" of glue building on the bow. This is caused by the glue cooling. Just wet your fingers in hot water and run them over the "globs" to smooth /remove them.

I use the pan of cool water (holding the bow and soaking the threads) to rinse my fingers as I go along...which is often. And it's a good idea to keep old rags/paper towels handy to wipe with and not ma's good towels.

When I'm satisfied with the job, I then smooth the entire surface with fingers dipped in hot water. At the tips, and all "low" spots, where the threads might have the tendency to pull loose while drying, take a sinew thread and tie it down.

The threads can have overlapped at the grips all they may. It won't hurt a thing as there is no bend there.

Take the sinewed bow and hang it from pegs/nails and leave it be. Here in N.E. Kansas with high humidity, I leave it right at two weeks to cure. A coupla bows that I made in the deserts of Las Vegas, I was satisfied with the cure in seven days. The color of the sinew will lighten noticeably as it dries.

The freshly sinewed bow

Don't even be tempted to try to pull the bow and see how it's doing before you are sure that it is cured. You will only succeed in breaking the all important bond between glue and wood.

When it is cured you will find that the drying, shrinking sinew has pulled the bow back...that's good. With Osage or White Oak, that is where it would remain, With our Hickory, it will still "follow the string" slightly...but not near as much as if we hadn't sinewed it.

When first pulling the bow...and probably for some time afterwards on the first few pulls, the glue will audibly crack. It will never cease to worry you!

When cured, the bow will probably need some final tillering. If everything had worked perfectly and the tillering was right on, you'd be in good shape. But most probably you will have to loosen one limb or the other. String the bow and pull it a few times...then lay it down and eyeball or measure it. If one limb bends more than the other, cut any sinew ties that may be in the way and carefully scrape or sand some wood from the BELLY of THE STIFFER of the limbs. Do this with the bow unstrung. Remove only a little and then string it...pull the bow a few times and then check it again. When both are equal (or close), the bow is all but done.

Some take the tillering to a more critical point. Using a board with notches cut into it about two inches apart, they place this board on the grip of the bow and move the string up a notch at a time, tillering at each step, until the draw length is reached. I've found that if the bow seems closely tillered as I've stated, it will look good all of the way out. At least I've had no problems.

One Hickory bow that I made several years ago, I got to tillering and really over did it. What began as a 55 lb. bow, because of overtillering first one limb and then the other, ended up as a 35 pounder. Instead of taking an ax to it as I was sorely tempted, I let it sit for a coupla weeks until I had calmed down. I then just re-sinewed it...a lot...and ended up with a fine shooting 55 lb bow. So much for the power of sinew.

O.K....The bow is sinewed, cured and tillered. Now take a knife or some sandpaper and go over all unsinewed parts of the belly and sides to remove any remnant of glue (just to make it pretty). Also, replace any ties that you removed while tillering.

But now something has to be done to protect the bow. Not only the wood (of which I spoke earlier) but also the sinew and the hide glue. Remember...this is all water soluble. If we were to lay the bow in a tub of water, before too long the glue would dissolve and the threads would all fall off. No good that!

It's best to figure that on rainy days, the bow will stay at home. When it rained, the Indians went home. And that's just about the truth. The bow was no good in wet weather. Even if it wasn't sinew backed, the strings, which were mostly of sinew or rawhide, were worthless.

The most common method of protecting the sinewed bow in days of old was to coat it liberally with grease, with some brains maybe thrown in for good measure. The smell? Well, I don't do mine that way.

I have coated some with a spar varnish...which didn't seem to hurt the sinew at all, but I just didn't like the brand new shiny look of a factory made bow on my completely hand made primitive piece. I now coat all of my bows liberally with a paste wax. This coats both the wood and the sinew...and the finish I can control.

I have read in one source of intestines being used to cover the bow for protection.

I have read in two sources, of the skins of serpents (most notably rattle-snakes) being used for the same.

I have looked hard at old bows all of my life whenever I have come close to them. They fascinate me. Since I have begun to make them, I look even more diligently...taking notes and photographs. In the last coupla years I have looked at well over 100 original bows. This includes the bows on display at the Smithsonian Institution in Wash. D.C., The Museum Of the Plains Indians in Cody, Wyo. and at museums and National Historic Sites too numerous too mention. Of all the bows that I have seen, probably about half of them were sinew backed... and NOT ONE OF THEM had either intestine or snake skin covering And that figure does not include the Smithsonian report of 1893 by Otis Mason on Bows, Arrows and Quivers...of the 43 bows illustrated, most are sinew backed...but not one is covered.

These coverings DO work. They are just NOT museum quality. I personally like the neat lines of the sinew backing and I don't like to cover, what is to me, a part of the beauty and labor of my hand made bow.

STRING

It's about time now, I guess, to make a string for the bow.

The best natural material to use here, which is what the Indians thought also, is sinew or rawhide. The various vegetable fibers are not strong enough for this task...though some will work for lighter weight bows.

This past season I was informed by two different people that one of the better bow strings could be made from the neck skin of a large turtle. I was informed that unlike sinew or rawhide, this won't stretch when wet. "Case skin" (like pulling a sock inside out) the neck and cut the cord spirally (like a barber pole), stretch it and allow it to dry. This now is all that I can tell you about it as I've never seen one nor tried it myself...yet. I certainly will, first chance that I get.

Deer rawhide makes for a good, strong, long lasting string. Cut it in a strip about a quarter inch wide from a circle of good solid rawhide. Begin cutting around the outside of this circle and continue until you get to the center. A surprisingly small piece will give a lot of lace. Then soak the cut lacing until it's pliable, double it and twist it tightly...stretching it out to let it dry. For heavier bows I will prepare the lace the same, but then I will "cord" it...making for an even stronger string. Again, do this while it is wet and stretch it to dry. Remember...the finished string will only be as strong as the weakest spot there-in...avoid thin spots and "scores".

Sinew was probably the favorite bow string of old. It was not only strong, but because of it's slightly elastic characteristic, gives an additional "snap" to the arrow as it is released. Use the leftover threads from backing your bow...or prepare them specifically for this. It is important to keep the threads as close to the same size as possible. One end of the thread will be thicker than the other, so alternate as you splice in to keep the finished product even. I begin "cording" with two threads, staggered so that the ends don't meet. You don't want the splices to adjoin as this will weaken the whole. Threads should also be soaked to make the "cording" easier.

Double this "two ply" and begin cording. Kink the thread, not evenly in half, between the thumb and forefinger of the left hand (for right handers)...twist the individual "two ply" strands tightly in one direction and then twist this in the other direction over the other individual "two ply" strand. (This sounds confusing as all hell, but read it slowly and carefully, and you should be able to follow it). Thus your "two ply" will become a "four ply" cord. Splice in threads as you proceed. (Cording is covered extensively in my book "PRIMITIVE FIRE AND CORDAGE").

THE ARROW

Now, up to this point, everything can have been done perfectly...but, if the arrow is not made properly, it will not fly true. Then you might just as well sharpen the end of the bow and use it as a spear. Yes, everything so far is important but if anything is to be considered "all important" here, it would be the arrow. If it won't fly consistently to where you want it, it's worthless. So MUCH care should be spent in the manufacture there-of.

Here again I will stress that this is the way that I make MY arrows. Not only do they work, but they are museum quality Plains Indian Arrows. I take a few extra steps here that are not necessary for you to end up with good quality shooters...and I'll tell you which ones that you can skip over and still end up with a suitable product...and I'll also stick in, where ever, other methods of ending up with the same. I spend from 10 to 12 hours making each arrow.

The materials that can be used for the shaft are many. The main requirements are that it be strong enough to sustain the force of the bow shooting it... and to be straight. Any 3/8th to 5/8th inch limb/bush/shoot is a possible candidate. Something as flimsy as cattail stems can be used...and in the Southern parts of this country, reeds have been used extensively. As with any other project, the Indians of old used what was available to them. Though I have quite a variety of materials to choose from here (willow, chokecherry, ash cedar and more...some of these could be cut in lengths and then have arrow shafts split from them), I favor working with dogwood. It is abundant and makes up into real nice arrows. These I also cut in the dead of winter while the sap is down.

When cutting them, I look for shafts that are as straight and as knot free as possible. Extra time spent now in the selecting will more than pay for itself later on. For my shafts, I like them to be approx. 3/8th of an inch thick when I cut them. I finish mine out at 1/4 inch and by the time that I remove the bark from them, they are about just right...If they are too thick, then I have to spend extra time in removing wood down to size.

I bundle and tie the shafts in groups of 15 or so and hang them in the house to dry. Tying keeps them from warping too severely...in from two to four weeks, they are ready to work.

Bundle of shafts (l) and chosen shaft lying next to a
finished arrow (r)

Once you have the cured shafts, the basic steps to a finished arrow are:

1	scraping and sizing
2	preliminary straightening
3	sanding
4	cutting of notches
5	more straightening
*6	cutting of lightning grooves
7	attaching of point
8	straighten again
*9	crest (paint owners mark)
10	fletch (put feathers on)
11	seal

* marks the steps that you can skip. As you can see, lots of straightening here. With primitive arrows, straightening is something that you will be doing for the life of the arrow.

Arrowmaking tools--sanding block, knife, bone sizer/wrench and jawbone for straightening wrench once arrow is finished

The first thing to do is to study the shaft...determine the length of the finished arrow, and place this with-in the shaft. All my shafts have knots. Where ever a leaf has grown has left a knot...a site that will always tend to warp. If possible, I try to place the arrow where no knot will be in the areas that will have feathers of sinew ties (this is not always possible though). Knots are prone to future warping and you will not be able to heat the area to re-straighten it if it has been covered. So it do help to watch the placement there-of. Once this is determined, I cut the shaft to length. I don't worry about which end is point or nock as I will work the entire length to the same size anyhow.

Using the edge of a sharp knife or a piece of flint, begin to scrape the shaft, beginning at the point end. Work an area about four to six inches long, constantly turning the shaft as you work. When I am able to run the bone sizer up the shaft, I'll work up another coupla inches or so until I finally reach the nock end. I like the sizer to fit loosely over the shaft because when the shaft

133

is heated to straighten, it will swell slightly and I use the same tool for straightening.

As I approach the nock end of the arrow, I cut around the shaft and leave the last 1/4 inch or so of the shaft the original size, sometimes leaving the bark on. This, done in a variety of ways, was common to many of the arrows of old. For the most part, the American Indian didn't use the Mediterranean (white mans) style of release, but actually pinched the nock of the arrow between thumb and forefinger and so needed something to grip. It also strengthens the arrow at this point against the force of the string.

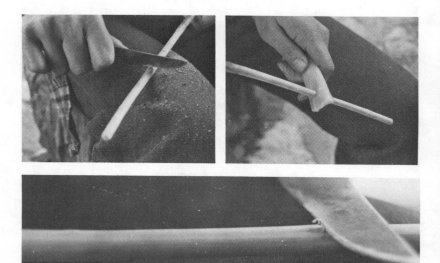

Scraping shaft (l)   Sizing shaft (r)   Carefully shaving any high knots (bottom)

To look down the shaft now, you will see that it ain't as straight as it might be...lotsa bumps, bends and cricks. Really not too pretty. But it do get better...soon.

We now will heat and straighten the shaft using the same bone tool that was used in sizing. The same process for heating the bow applies here...slowly and carefully. The slightest scorch here will tell....when the arrow hits something solid, it will break. I normally work three or more arrows at a time so that when I heat and straighten one, it cools while I work on the others, and it is cooled enough by the time that I get back to it that I don't have to worry about re-bending areas that I've already worked. (Got that?). Take your time. Get the arrow as straight as you can. With some of the poorer shafts, this may take some doing, but stick with it. The bumps of knots will look like hell right now, but just kinda look "through" them...get the main part of the shaft straight. Remember to keep lots of grease on the shaft to help against scorching. It will only take a minute or so to get the shaft hot enough to bend.

Once straight...as straight as you can get it, you can (or not, as you wish), wash the grease off with hot water and detergent. This is only to prevent it from building up in the sand stone/paper in the next step. I don't.

This next step, sanding, will do wonders for your cricked shaft. Using two pieces of sandstone about 5 to 6 inches long with a groove cut for the shaft...or with a 2x2 block of wood the same length , cut in half length wise and with grooves cut for the shaft AND SANDPAPER, place the shaft in the groove and run it several times through this...almost magically, the "cricked" stick will take on the appearance of a lathe turned dowel. The length of the shaft smoother first cuts the high spots of knots and other bad spots, leaving the lower parts untouched. After repeating this several times, brushing the stone or paper in between to keep it clean, the shaft makes a wonderful transformation.

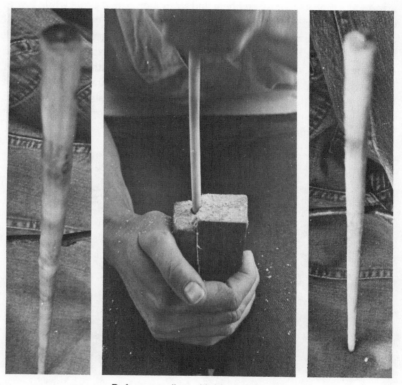

Before, sanding with block and after

Now return to the fire and grease/heat and straighten again. You should have a fine looking shaft.

Many of the "old" arrows had grooves cut from the base of the feathers to the point, sometimes two but more commonly three. These were but slight cuts made lengthwise along the shaft with knife, stone or bone...sometimes straight...sometimes wavy and sometimes with zig-zags...or any combination there-of. The true purpose of these has been lost. Some refer to them as blood grooves...others lightning grooves. Whatever, if you want them, now is the time to put them in.

Cutting the groove to fit the arrowhead can take a number of approaches. In some situations, you may want only to sharpen and fire harden the tip. (I always think of fire hardening as only removing whatever moisture remains in the wood?). Or you may want to splice in a blunt tip, easily enough done and deadly on small game. But for large game, we'll want a more appropriate "cutting" point. Bone or stone may be used...(preparation there-of to be covered in a later book), in which case, especially for the stone point, some custom sawing/fitting will be in order. I use either a hacksaw, or just as often, a serrated piece of flint, to saw into the tip of the shaft. This, in conjunction with a SHARP knife, can snug an awkward piece in little time.

Most commonly, though, because of modern game laws, metal points will be used. About any sheet metal will make a serviceable point...scrap metal, part of an old fender, or, as I commonly use, a barrel hoop. A hacksaw and a file will give you a point of your choosing.

The resulting metal points can usually be mounted snugly with-in a saw cut.

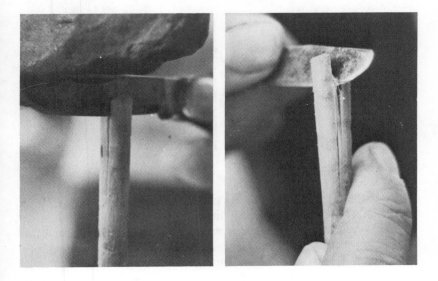

The more common approach in a primitive situation would be to carefully split the shaft for an inch or so up the middle, and then to cut the sides to fit the point. Securing the point with glue and sinew will reinforce the split.

Whatever type of point or method of cutting, I always seat the point with hide glue. It dries harder than the wood and really reinforces. I finish it all off with a good wrapping of sinew. (Remember cross referencing...pine pitch can be used for glue...or none at all. And in lieu of sinew, there are vegetable fibers galore in nature that would suffice).

Now also cut the nock for the string. You will see from the photos how I do mine. No special advice needed here...just to fit the string.

137

I have read in two accounts that the Indians cut the notch for the string parallel to the arrowhead for hunting purposes and at 90 degrees from it for war purposes. This was supposedly to allow the arrowhead to slide more readily between the ribs of whatever game he was after. I personally think that this is a lot of bunk...the arrow, as soon as it leaves the string, is spinning, if ever so slightly. But, I do make mine to conform to "hunting".

Now is a good time to wash the arrow to remove any oils and/or grease...especially where the feathers will be applied.

If so desired, now is also the time to paint, or crest, the arrow. In days gone by, this was done to show who belonged to the meat...or scalp. Sort of the owners signature.

Sawing of notch in nock with serrated obsidian

Fletching...the applying of feathers to stabilize the arrow in flight. This can be a real pain, but is pretty much a necessity.

A simple method shown to me be an arrow maker and flintknapper, was to simply tie two feathers, one on either side of the shaft, at the "point" end, allowing the back end to simply lie alongside the shaft. Though I haven't done this myself, I've seen it work ...well. In a primitive situation, this would be the cat's meow.

I do things a bit more complicated. I work generally with wild turkey feathers...tail if I have them, wing otherwise, Choose three feathers with all having the same bend (same wing or same side of the tail). Three feathers will do two arrows.

To prepare, pound gently the quill portion the entire length of the feather...this will allow it to split more readily. Then using a knife, bone or stone tool, split it evenly the entire length. All of one side of the feathers for one arrow...the other side for another. We are trying to keep everything as equal as possible.

Two smaller goose feathers secured only at bottom

Now cut the feathers of one arrow to the same length. Mine are made between five and six inches long...not necessary. Whatever length that you like. Trim the vane up at both ends for about 1/2 inch for tying to the shaft, and also trim the entire feather vane to about 3/8th of an inch...actually, the longer the feather, the narrower the vane. Use a sharp knife to trim the bottom of the quill (the part to fit to the shaft) so that the feather will lie flat. If it has any tendency to curl in one direction, cut through the quill ONLY ON THE INSIDE OF THE CURL where ever necessary...just get it to lie flat with the vanes pointed up. Finish off by sanding the bottom of the quill smooth. Some remove the pith of the quill...I don't. Finally, taper and smash the lower portion of the quill so that when it leaves the bow it will run smoothly over your hand and the bow.

Carefully splitting feather

Now comes the "funnest" part... attaching the damn things to the shaft in some semblance of order. It can try the patience of most...especially me.

One vane will be applied at a 90 degree angle to the notch of the nock...the other two placed at equal distances from that. This allows the two "bottom" feathers to run smoothly over the bow. Most color the upper vane differently so as to be able to place it in the string more quickly...the majority of "old" arrows were not...so I don't. Begin by running a sinew thread, wetted, around the shaft about a half inch below the nock, tieing down first the "up" feather. Then with additional revolutions around the shaft, tieing down the other two....pulling and pushing with fingernails the feathers so that they are in proper position before wrapping tight...and then seal the thread with a drop or two of hide glue to hold it all in place.

When this has been accomplished, begin again with the "up" feather at the other end and pull that smooth against the shaft and begin wrapping with another sinew thread. Here, unlike the upper tie, do not let the sinew thread run UNDER any of the feathers. Remember that this is the end that will have to run "into" your hand and the bow as it is released. The smoother that this is kept, the better. So tie all three of the feathers at the same time, wrap a coupla times with the thread, but before you get it too tight, using your fingernails, rotate the feathers so that they lie straight with the shaft...a coupla more tighter wraps...and then take the edge of your knife and "bite" it into the end of the quill and pull on it ever so gently so as to pull the vane tight, and it will then lie pretty much flat on the shaft. If you pull too hard, it is possible to pull the upper end out from it's tie.

141

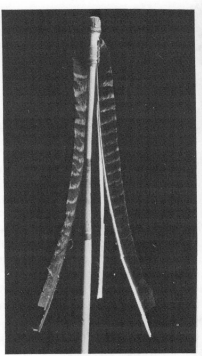

Fletching tied at top (above)
Tied top and bottom (r)

The arrow should now look like an arrow....soooooo pretty. If done as I've described, museum quality. It is now ready to use...but.

I believe that the arrows of "old" were about 50/50 in the feathers being left as is or having been glued down. Myself, I prefer to glue them down. So if that's what you want, melt down a small batch of hide glue and HOT water...just a bit of water here. It's best if the glue sets up fast...the thicker, the better. With a pointed stick apply a bead of glue to each side of the feathers...If they bow away from the shaft a bit, they can be held in gently with the fingers till the glue sets.

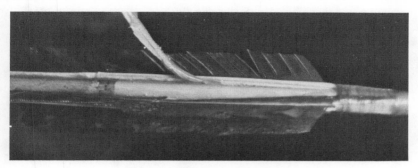

Glueing down of fletching

Top view of fletching

When all of the glues have set up good, just a coupla hours, it is wise to go over the entire shaft with a paste wax. I would use wax in lieu of a varnish because you will more than likely have to reheat and straighten the shaft in the future.

What has just been described makes for a damn fine arrow. But you can make an equally serviceable one by not adding all the little touches that make this a museum quality piece. In a truly primitive situation, I certainly wouldn't

143

worry myself with lightning grooves, cresting, fancily applied feathers or perfectly sized shafts. I WOULD concentrate on a "true" shaft, so that it would fly straight...a point of sorts (only need to penetrate the chest cavity of any critter and it'll be dead...a sharpened stick would do that)...nothing fancy...and some sort of fletching. Any feather would work...even a strip of carefully crafted bark.

Our finished arrow with two others

(Following Page)

The finished sinew backed hickory bow, 45 inches long, tops my 50 lb. scale at 17 inches--leaving me with probably about an 80 lb. bow with my 22 inch arrow, (bottom).

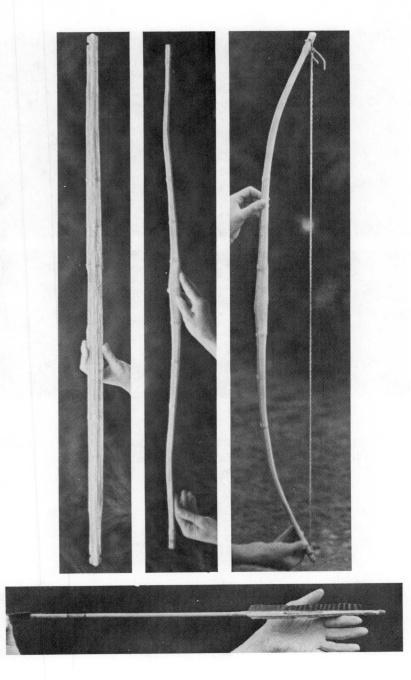

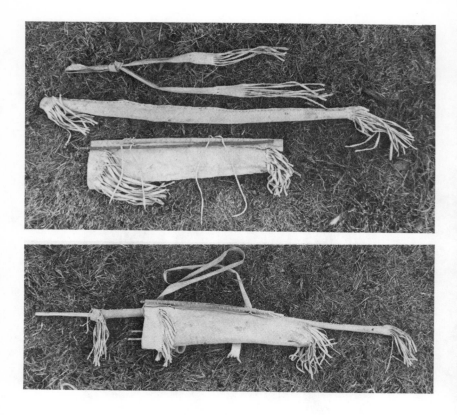

Top, layout of pieces of a "typical hunting" bow case/quiver of the Plains. Bottom of quiver is rawhide sewn in with sinew.
Bottom, all together

4

Makin' Meat-2

Obtaining Subsistence in Nature
Deadfalls/Snare/Fishtrap/Atlatl & more

INTRODUCTION

"Makin' Meat". Since the publication of my last book, *"Makin' Meat - 1"*, I've had many questions as to what the title means. The early mountain men of the American west used this term to note that they had obtained subsistence...mostly in the fact that they had shot some game animal. "This child shore had starvin' times for nigh on ten days afore he made meat". This could be interpreted to mean that the speaker had spent 10 days with no nourishment...and then had either shot something...trapped something...knocked a bird silly with a rock...or even found a half-eaten/rotted carcass left by some wolves. I hope that this will explain the title to the non-buckskinner.

Within this volume (Volume?...let's be realistic, booklet)...OK then, booklet, we will delve into various methods of obtaining subsistence in the wilderness. *"Makin' Meat-1"* (MM-1) dealt with making the bow and arrow from nature...and then we ran out of space. Actually, the bow and arrow is quite a ways up the ladder when it comes to primitive gathering.

I'll begin this book with a trapline...the first thing that an experienced woodsperson would pursue if and/or when placed in a primitive situation. On our line you'll note that most of the sets will be for small critters such as mice/rats/ rabbits/birds. This is because it's an initial primitive situation; that is, what one would be depending upon for life. Small things will keep us going. Large critters will be a bonus. We'll also set a coupla fish type traps.

At this point let me point out...SOME OR ALL OF THE TRAP TYPES THAT I WILL SHOW WILL BE ILLEGAL IN MANY...OR POSSIBLY MOST...STATES IN THE UNION. CHECK YOUR LOCAL REGULATIONS.

ALSO...ONE OF THE TRIGGER MECHANISMS THAT I WILL BE SHOWING YOU IS EASILY CAPABLE OF BEING SET TO HURT/MAIM/KILL LARGE GAME, INCLUDING THE HUMAN SPECIES. What I will be showing will be how one is fully capable of subsisting in a truly primitive or SURVIVAL situation. Some of the traps if left set could be detrimental to the well being of your neighbors' cats/dogs/children. USE CAUTION!!

Now back to the line. It will also be mentioned how and where to place some of the sets so as to possibly (actually quite possibly) catch some of the larger species of game..from which besides just nourishment you would be able to set aside furs, skins, sinew, bones, etc.

One big thing here is to think small. Mice, packrats, minnows, crawdads, insects...all will sustain life. If you were to approach your primitive situation thinking only of larger game, you just might well starve.

Something else to think about. You could eat the meat of wild game for weeks on end...and starve. Wild game is not marbled with fat as is our usual diet of domesticated meat.

You may have to break prejudices of eating habits that you have. In a primitive situation, especially if it's a case of survival, you may have no choice what goes thru your mouth. Basically, the hair/skin and intestines will go out...the rest will go in, except larger bones...and then you will want to roast/boil the larger bones and remove the marrow. Cooking methods we will approach in another book.

A story that I read somewhere. During the last century a ship was ice locked in the Arctic and the crew was taken in by the natives. Come spring, all but one (or two) were dead and the authorities at first thought that the Intuits had murdered them...until it came to light that the white man ate only the red meat...where the natives ate about the entire animal. Stomach contents and the marrow of the bone didn't appeal to the whites...and they starved to death with full stomachs. Just something else for you to be thinking about before taking to the wilds...also hope that your critter hasn't been munching on poison ivy/oak or sumac. Ouch!!!

Various plants can make up much of the diet...and I can't go into that...as my knowledge on this is extremely limited. There are many guides on the market to fill your appetite for edible plants (no pun intended).

Long before the bow and arrow came along, man was plenty content with an apparatus called the atlatl...a spear thrower. As with the hand drill for making fire, this worked so well that there was no real rush to better what was at hand. BUT...once the bow was thought up...both for the drill and the arrow...the old ways were quickly set aside. Progress...damn!

Well, I don't pretend to be any expert with the atlatl (nor with the hand drill), but I do have one of my own making and also know the components and why it works...mostly...enough to be able to guide you in making one of your own. Besides, they are faster to make than a good bow...deadly on large game with-in range...and a lot of fun. So you'll also learn about this.

Once there is enough meat on hand in your camp...we'll show you the old, natural way of preserving it. <u>Do remember though...if you get bad meat...bad tallow...bad berries, I assume no responsibility for bad bellies</u>.

That should be about enough to fill these allotted 48 pages. In my next book maybe we'll go into the various methods of cooking some of this stuff up...with no white man stuff.

April 1988

THE TRAP LINE

One thing that about all outdoorsmen/woodsmen/survivalists will agree on is the fact that the trap line is the MOST expedient method of keeping a supply of meat on hand with a minimum of effort.

If, for some reason, you are on the move, a few, or several traps might be set out each night. But if you are in a good area which supplies all of your needs (food source/water/shelter) and decide to spend some time in one location, then here you would set out one or more "lines". By line, I mean a certain number of traps set in any given location...up a certain creek...along a certain ridge...south of camp...north of camp, etc.

I'll only mention a few "tips" as it comes to trapping. Trapping is a profession in itself and there are numerous books on the market to teach one the art of trapping any particular type of critter that one decides to specialize in. The same with hunting techniques. I can't begin to teach you the years of knowledge necessary to become "one" with nature...that's up to you. I'll give you the tools and information necessary to begin. It's up to you to apply them, but you will have to be aware that you can't catch it if it ain't there - look for <u>fresh</u> signs and trap/hunt accordingly.

Also, here, with the deadfall and snare, I'll show you ONE (actually, now three) trigger system. There are several that are shown, and shown, and shown, in several "survival" type and outdoors books. I've tried several of them. NONE work to the satisfaction that I desire...and most are, I believe, just perpetuated myths. They look good on paper and "sometimes" work—and so are included in any/all books dealing with this subject. I thought for a long time on how I was going to be able

152

to get a 80 to 100 pound rock to fall where I wanted it to and when it was supposed to-<u>NEARLY 100% of the time.</u> AND yet be simple enough to set that the entire time, from making the trigger to finished set, took only a few minutes.

I've spent the last year showing the trigger system that I came up with to any/all outdoorsmen that I came across. No one has yet been able to say that they knew of it...and all agreed that it do work.

So pay attention to the accompanying photos and what I say...go out to your back yard and make it work. My first set...from the initial inspiration to completed working dead-fall with a 123 pound rock, took right at 20 minutes. Your first should take no more time than this.

For to make this work, you will need bout 12 to 15 inches of cordage (Primitive Fire and Cordage will show you this).

You'll see from the photos that the trigger needs to be shaved down somewhat at one end..to hold it in the knot of cordage on the other piece of the trigger.

Well....hell, I'm not even gonna try to describe in words this system. We'll just wait for the photos and then write the cutlines. It's really hard to describe this with only words...and actually the photos won't even need words, which you can see.

MY trigger system..so simple...so easy to construct under a primitive wilderness situation. And so effective.

THE MOST efficient part of this trigger is that it is set BEFORE you position your 100 pound-plus rock...in this case 123 pounds.

The baited, set trigger. A scrap piece of meat held to the trigger by cordage. Note how the trigger fits into the cordage tied around the stick driven into the ground. Round on round. The slightest "busying" of the bait will release it all.

Note that a separate piece of cordage is tied to the weight-holding stick, to <u>pull</u> it when the spring releases. Initially I used the spring stick to PUSH the upright out...but here the spring is less likely to push away your supper along with the stick. ALWAYS REMEMBER...to use dead/dry sticks for the spring sticks. Green sticks will conform to the bend and lose their "spring".

TOP: Deadfall set for packrat. The baited trigger is placed on the left side of the underside of the rock and the left side is blocked by another upright rock...so that when triggered, the animal must travel futher to escape.
BOTTOM: Three mornings later...meat! - and, yes-this packrat we ate.

LEFT: Deadfall set near packrat house. UPPER RIGHT: Three mornings later, the tripped trap and LOWER RIGHT: Bingo!...meat!

The same trigger system set as a snare. Bait is on the trigger..noose is on the ground. Many, many applications for this.

Woodland trail set snare...can you spot it?

LEFT: Trail set snare...note trigger. RIGHT: Trail kinda blocked to help guide the critter through the noose. Of the three mornings that I had this set, it was tripped once, with the noose drawn up but no evidence of any critter...and the other two mornings the noose had been disturbed by passing animals. The noose needs to be JUST the right size...too large, animals will run through it...too small, they will only push it aside.

SURPRISE...in this morning's mail an envelope from Steve Watts...primitive skills instructor for the Schiele Museum of Natural History, Gastonia, North Carolina. I here quote his note. "John - hope all is well with you. I just ran across this deadfall trigger (a new one to me)-It's like greased lightning. Got it from Henry Rhyne (a local old time trapper). Henry say's that he got it from a trapper in Alaska in the 1940's. Says it was mostly used for birds. You might already know it-but as I say, it was a new one on me. Take care-Keep it up. Steve".

Well Steve...and folks...it's also a new one for me...and it do work. Steve and I have been in correspondence for a while...mostly just sharing notes. Of all my inquiring about deadfall triggers...and of all the folks that I ran into last season...this is one that works. Steve's initial response to my inquiry was that he knew only the old standbys (that I don't mention here because of the percentage of failures)...and then this in today's mail. Neat!!! So now you have another GOOD usable trigger. Where this would come in the handiest over the other is on HARD surfaces where driving the second trigger piece into the ground would be out of the question.

PRECEDING PAGE:
TOP: Stout snare set at pond....snares (3) were set out on the ground from baited trigger...here it is better to use triggers of about one inch diameter rather than the illustrated 1/4 inch. BOTTOM: Geri hauling in drowned possom.

The four views of the trigger sent me by Steve Watts should be self-explanatory. Bait is placed under rock, or live box. The slightest downward pressure to the stick releases it all...as Steve says, "like greased lightning". Bait can be placed on end of stick or ground...as birds will perch on it to eat.

164

Geri and I just got back from a week's "Cave Man's Convention" in central Oregon, hosted by Jim Riggs and Brian James. What a great sharing of primitive skills...mostly, but far from all, dealing with flint knapping. One of the "other" tips gleaned was Jim's old standby Paiute dead fall trigger system. This do work...but with much difficulty when setting heavy falls for large game (the same applies to the second trigger sent by Steve). But when setting out MANY traps in your line, you can't know too many triggers. Where one might be just the checker for a particular set, another might not be at all usable. Pick and choose just what works best for your situation as it arises.

FOLLOWING PAGE
Looky--another goodie from Jim Riggs. Paiute deadfall trigger. TOP: Jim Riggs checking out my work. BOTTOM: Front view. Study carefully the two photos...they show all that is needed to construct your own. The upright and horizontal trigger pieces and the cordage are all the same length. The short piece tied (or thru loop) to cordage needs to be stiff. The lower thin piece going from that to the bottom of the rock could be a stout stem of grass...so little force is applied to it. Bait is placed where the thin stick (or stem of grass) touches the rock.

Jim's only comment about my setting of this was that the upright should NOT be under the rock just in case the horizontal fails to kick it free. When touched at bait, though, the rock fell as it was designed to. Also, not really visible but very important, is the slight groove cut into the top of the upright to hold the horizontal.

I have always believed in the power of photographs but with these traps we have had some questions posed as to their construction - so we are now including line drawings of three to help clarify.

The only change you will note is with the construction of the Paiute deadfall (page 21&22)... the trigger I have always touted as the easiest and fastest to make but the hardest and most time consuming to set - so we seldom, if ever, used it. BUT ...

... exasperation finally got me to experimenting ... two changes and our trapping world turned over. Now this trap is what we use for our bread and butter. Fast & easy not only to construct but *now* also to set. With basic instructions, we have had ten and twelve year olds setting them in just minutes. And it *has* been proven in the field.

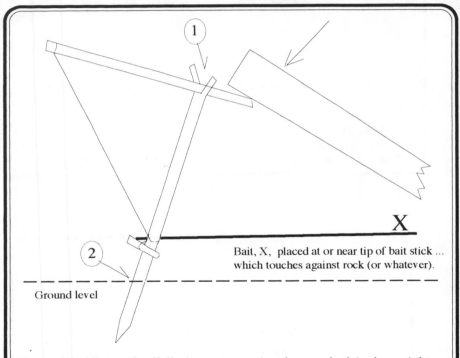

1

2

X

Bait, X, placed at or near tip of bait stick ... which touches against rock (or whatever).

Ground level

The modified Paiute deadfall trigger. two major changes, both in the upright stick. 1) Use of a natural "Y" to support the horizontal piece and 2) pushing the upright into the ground to stabilize it ... this being the most critical change. Just insure that the upright is far enough out to prevent the weight from falling onto it or even brushing against it which will slow it down. For most efficiency, keep the two wood pieces at approx. 90° angle - which will keep the string at approx. 45°.

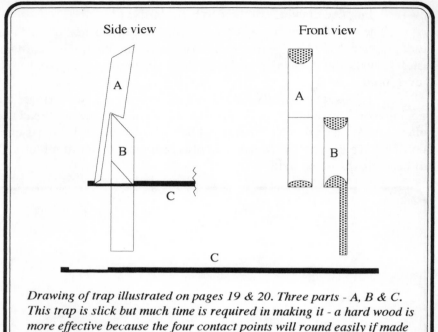

Drawing of trap illustrated on pages 19 & 20. Three parts - A, B & C. This trap is slick but much time is required in making it - a hard wood is more effective because the four contact points will round easily if made from softer woods ... and once rounded, it becomes a real trick to set.

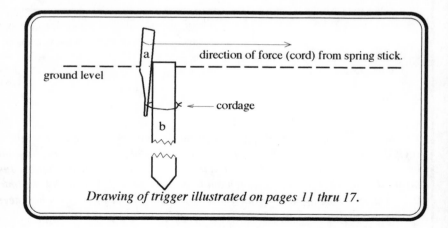

Drawing of trigger illustrated on pages 11 thru 17.

The following trap was originally printed as a supplement in book number 5, **PRIMITIVE WILDERNESS COOKING METHODS**. It was shown to us by Gordon Nagorski of Ontario, Canada.

The basic set-up as shown (L) from the front quarter and from (R) the side. This is a cubby set so the front will be the entrance.

(L) A close-up of the trigger and (R) the other end of the trigger.

The set-up (before making "step" on bottom stick/trigger). Study closely how this is put together referring back to the close-up of the upper part of the trigger. A single piece of cordage is looped around the deadfall log and over, very near the rounded tip, of the trigger...and the bottom of the trigger is held by a stick going crosswise between the slanted pieces stuck into the ground (and tied at the top). A cord is run from the cross stick to the step stick (bottom trigger), tieing it above the ground so that stepping on it pulls the top cross out releasing the upper trigger and log.

170

(L) Sticks placed on bottom trigger to form step and (R) bark placed over that for re-inforcement/firmness.

The set made into a cubby. Bait is placed beyond the "step". Two smaller logs can be placed at the front so that the deadfall log will fall between...thereby, hopefully, breaking the back of the trapped critter. Distance from where the "dead falls" (ha, gotcha there) to the step is critical. Remember that the animal's front legs will be on the "step"...and place accordingly so that his mid-back is under falling log.

Geri pushes on the "step" and it all comes tumbling down....fast! Note trigger (circled, upper center) flying off.

O.K., now you've got a working knowledge of three GOOD WORKING trigger systems that are really simple to put together in a primitive situation. Let's set up a line.

Remember, think small. If by chance (in most parts of the country a good chance), you have in the area a packrat's house...this would be a great place to set as many as six, or even more sets. Here a family unit might run as many as six to eight critters. Packrats are a reasonably good sized animal and worthy of your attention. Just look for sign that the house is occupied (fresh tracks/scat, etc.) and set wherever is convenient. Rats are inquisitive and you won't need anything fancy to attract them to your set. Any scraps from a previous kill will work as bait...or some grass seed chewed up well and made into a paste. That'll get you started. We've even had deadfalls tripped by rats chewing through the cordage—maybe after the gease residue left by our fingers?

Most of the critters that we're now looking for will leave definite trails in their wake. Rabbits/mice/etc., will use the same runs time and again...very visible to the naked eye in the grass and leaves. These will lead to good trail sets for snares...or just off the trail for baited deadfalls and snares.

If the "right" pool of water is available you can put out a stout snare. Most all critters that you are trapping will eat your snare material (if you are using natural fiber cordage)..and actually do include it in their daily diet. You need to kill...or in this case preoccupy them with staying afloat, so that they won't (hopefully) consider turning around and biting your cordage in two...give them a chance to drown.

A REAL reason to use DEADfalls in lieu of snares whenever possible. Even if you were to catch a rabbit by the hind foot and he wasn't able to reach the cordage (unlikely)...the ruckus that he would make would attract a

173

coyote/fox, etc. and your dinner would be gone come morning. So...a good lesson here. DEADfall whenever possible.

Another idea for BIG meat with a snare (of course, you can see just how you could easily construct a deadfall of any size using the first trigger system illustrated). If you've ever spent time around a campfire in the woods, you've surely heard noises just outside of the circle of light...or maybe even seen eye's reflected in the light...or seen fresh tracks around (and sometimes inside) the perimeter the next morning of coyotes, raccoons, deer, large cats, etc. A snare on the ground with a trip cord hooked to the trigger or a baited snare set just MIGHT get you a larger critter tied up (excuse the pun) just long enough for you to grab your club or spear and enable you to apply a fatal wound. Just here...USE CAUTION. Have a torch ready or some light source. I'd hate to run blindly into the dark and try to knock a mountain lion or bear, Griz or Black, on the head with a stick. And remember also the legalities involved. You MIGHT get away with these tricks in a survival situation...but on a weekend campout I doubt that your local fish and game commission would turn their heads whilst you practice your survival skills. Do your practicing on rats and rabbits.

Set yourself up several lines. Each line might have as many as fifty or as few as eight or ten sets. Each situation/locale will be different. Once the lines are in place, it will take only a glance to check each set...and to re-set if necessary, only a moment or two more.

Also, all the time that you are in the primitive situation, remember that you'll also be "gathering"...materials for cordage/fire making/bow staves/arrow shafts/workable stone/bones...anything to make life a little easier.

Now, let's not forget about our feathered friends. I don't know of any birds that you <u>can't</u> eat (though you better not take my word for that and maybe do some research on this), but there are some that I would prefer <u>not</u> to eat under <u>normal</u> circumstances....I <u>ONCE</u> tried coot!

But birds, the same as rodents, are food...protein...something to keep you going. The deadfall trigger sent by Steve Watts, as he mentions, is superb, and probably primarily designed for birds. Our heavier duty deadfall trigger shown will easily get your crows and/or raptors (raptors are protected federally) because meat can be used as a bait...though in most of our sets, the bait is hidden from the view of birds.

A net is an ideal way to get all types of birds. The one shown is very loosely "woven"...not "netted"...but will catch and hold all birds...as they will naturally spread their wings and become further entangled. The net shown is approx. three and a half feet square and can be triggered by the bird (as shown) or the watching trapper can just let go of the cord and drop it on the birds whenever he has a full enough house. By manually releasing the net, the net itself is assured relief from a lot of damage if catching a large bird/coon/possum/coyote. Though the net might hold any of the above (especially a turkey/duck, etc.), it wouldn't for very long. Any of these critters would make short work of your net...which will require many long hours on your part to assemble. If you were to drop it on a bird...or birds...or critter...a quick run over and a thump on the head with a club (or wringing of their necks)...will keep them from damaging the net.

Trigger for the bird net. Notched and will be securely
lashed.

Two views showing "set" trigger. Note in right photo how cordage
runs from trigger thru crossed stakes...from there up over tripod back
to net.

NEXT PAGE

TOP: The set bird net. Study closely and follow cordage from trigger,
thru crossed sticks, over tripod (could be tree limb) and back to top of
net. The net itself serves as a "spring stick". With just the "slightest"
touch to the trigger, it all came tumbling down...(bottom)...quicker and
easier than I could ever have hoped for.

178

Also on the trap line, let's not forget about fish. If close to a water source that supports fish, the use of the impoundment shown will often corral you plenty of nourishment. You can also make a "minnow type" trap out of any straight shoots/limbs.

With some practice you can learn yourself to be fast enough to catch ahold of crawdads as you turn over rocks in river or stream. The tails of these are a delicacy. Frogs are not to be forgotten either.

And not really a trap, is the bank line. I have seen drawings of several types of primitive fishhooks...but from personal experience, I know just how much a fish will fight...and most of these makeshift hooks of bone and/or wood just won't normally hold up to the strain. One that does work is the straight piece of limber/hard (not brittle) wood or bone...kinda like a rounded toothpick is shaped with the line tied around the center. This is inserted into a minnow/small frog/insect/toad and hung from a LIMBER stick stuck into the bank. The bait/hook need be a little below water level - just enough slack to allow the fish to swallow the bait/hook. Even intestines/scrap meats/fats can be wrapped around the stick/hook. Fish will swallow this bait...once inside their body, the line, tied to the center of the hook, prevents it from being removed/regurgitated. If the cordage is strong enough so that the fish's teeth don't wear it through...you've got meat. If you are camped near a water source that will adapt to this, you should put dead leaves, etc. on the pole to alert you to the fact that there is a fish on so you can get to it immediately before its teeth cut through your cordage.

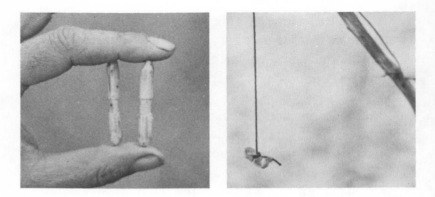

LEFT: A pair of "gorge" fish hooks...these made of green cedar for large catfish...smaller hooks for smaller fish. RIGHT: Baited with scrap meat and tied to cordage.

Bankline set (actually you can just barely see a 2nd)...limber poles stuck SECURELY into the bank...Geri making fish trap in background.

The same net that is shown for birds will also catch fish...except here make sure that all weavings of the cordage are tied (or learn to "net"—though this will require more cordage). The result is a gill net...and it do work. Fish swim into it and are got.

And while you're messing around the water, keep an eye out for fresh water clams. Maybe not as tasty as their salt water cousins, but they did sustain the early Indians. The muddy taste they have can be somewhat relieved by letting them sit in clean, fresh water for several days. My one experience with them left a bit to be desired...but in the primitive state I'm certain that they would improve in flavor considerably.

Well...that basically is what I have to offer here on traps. But do remember that the best made trap set will catch you nothing if it isn't set where the critters are. Learn to look for "signs"...and set accordingly.

NEXT PAGE

TOP PHOTO: A pretty simple yet very effective fish trap. It is here placed in the neck of a pond. Any shallow pool in a creek/river/lake would work...or in the riffles between pools of a creek. BOTTOM: Close up of how entrance to "trap" works. Very limber twigs, etc. allow fish to enter but prevent their leaving. This set was made without the use of any cordage..only interlacing the shoots. Scraps of fats/guts/etc. are placed within the enclosure...hoping to draw fish Check local regulations pertaining to fish traps-this is illegal in Kansas!

GATHERING

Now we'll go into some gathering, something that the primitive person will be doing from the moment that he becomes primitive. You will NEVER stop "gathering". Your only tools needed here will be the rabbit/throwing/digging stick, a sack or basket and knowledge of what to gather.

The "rabbit" stick is only a limb or other piece of hardwood, from 18 to 30 inches long (mine is 27 inches), heavy enough to go through grass when thrown at rabbits, birds or whatever...light enough to be thrown easily with force...and pointing it at one end will allow you to dig various roots and tubers.

This tool is amazingly effective.

Once you have become accustomed to throwing it accurately, you will have a fair chance of hitting a critter at up to 100 feet. You may spot a rabbit (look for his eye) before he dashes...or he often will run only a few yards and then stop...and often, once put to flight, a sudden yell or whistle

My personal throwing stick. To make this a rabbit stick, I need only to throw it at a rabbit. It makes quite a whooshing sound as it travels...thinning it somewhat would help that...from this the boomerang developed. Though a rock would go where this wouldn't through brush, on open ground, or in the air, this cuts a swath of 27 inches...so I need't be quite so accurate.

will stop them long enough for you to get a shot. And how often has one almost stepped on a pheasant or covey of quail before they took to flight...pheasants especially seem to hang in mid-air for several seconds allowing you a good chance for a hit at ten to fifteen yards. If you miss though, watch where your stick lands, not the bird, or you will lose both.

Turn over logs, rocks, etc. and if you are quick enough you will be able to club surprised mice, rats or lizards. Be cautious of snakes while doing this...but don't be afraid to club or stone one should he be found. I know of no snake that is not edible (but be sure to check this out if unsure)... but of course, with rattlesnakes, copperheads, water moccasins...leave the head alone...that is where the poison sacs are. The only other poisonous snake in North America is the coral snake, found primarily in the Southeast. I would NOT eat this snake until I was to learn more about it..it is a highly venomous snake whose venom effects the nervous system. Fortunately, one doesn't normally have to worry about being bitten by one because of its small size and mouth.

A sack or basket will be covered in a later book...but it really don't take much knowhow to put together some container in a well stocked woods...especially with a knowledge of cording (Primitive Fire and Cordage). A real simple weaving will make a tight enough sack from most any cordage material. And limber shoots of willow, dogwood, etc. will make a <u>simple</u> basket with no special skills/knowledge.

SEEDS and NUTS will be some of your most valuable additions to your diet. You may be wise to check which few are not edible (poison ivy/sumac/oak or whatever)...but most are O.K. In fact, much better than O.K. The nutritional value of seeds and nuts is amazing. (Here we are stepping somewhat out of the realm of my knowledge and into edible plants...so double check what I say here). Any grass seed will be welcome. Fruit seeds abound in nature. If in the timber, look for nuts (I can't stress enough that you will have to do your own research on edible plants, etc.). Acorns can have a bitter tannic removed by leaching several times in hot water...white oak have the sweetest acorns (I read that in several places). These all can be ground into a flour...added to soups/stews as is... many eaten raw. But these will be an important addition to your diet.

A tip given to me by a friend who had read it somewhere (take it for what it's worth). Tear apart a packrat's house (only in an emergency...it is his house)...maybe after having trapped it well...whatever. The packrat will have stored various seeds and tubers within. Also the downy beds will make great tinder for making your fire...dry under the wettest conditions. If you tear this apart while still occupied, keep your rabbit stick handy. When they first come out they will be really confused and slow to find shelter/cover. Make meat!

185

ATLATL

The ATLATL...or spear-thrower. What a beautiful and efficient tool/weapon...used for thousands of years before the discovery of the bow and arrow. And when one watches someone proficient with this tool, such as two world champions I know, one begins to understand just why the bow was so slow in coming of age.

Distance throws of seventy-plus yards are simple. Pie plate size accuracy at twenty to thirty yards not uncommon with practice...with all the force necessary to kill large game...bison and mastodon in days gone by!

The Atlatl (thrower) itself is not difficult to construct. As you can see in the photos, it's nothing more than a cheater..an extension of your arm...most averaging about 15 to 20 inches long. Not only does it extend your arm to create more force, it also takes that force and concentrates it at the END of the spear/dart...not in the middle as in the case of a hand thrown one. Noting photos at the time of release, (not included here) the spear actually bends from the force of the atlatl, thereby creating an additional force as the dart "snaps" away. And if the atlatl is fine tuned to the weight of the dart/spear that it is throwing, it will also have a light pliability to it which will also "snap" in tune with the dart/spear...creating that much more speed and force.

As with the arrow, most time will be spent with the spear/dart (I'll refer to it as the dart from here out). The darts run from four to seven feet in length...five to six being the more common. Much time will be spent in straightening it...as with the arrow (refer to my book *MM-1, the Primitive Bow and Arrow*).

Geri preparing to drop a Mastodon with atlatl.

LEFT The fuller fletching slowed darts considerably, trimming helped considerably. RIGHT: Closeup showing indents for nub to fit into.

Showing how atlatl mates with dart....this could be done just
the opposite...a round tip on the dart and a depression on the
atlatl for it to fit into.

Front and side views of my atlatl. The weight is to counterbalance the
weight and length of my darts...but I got a bit carried away and it is a
bit sluggish...but I do have the advantage of a built-in war club if I run
outta darts. Actually, most originals had no counterweight..

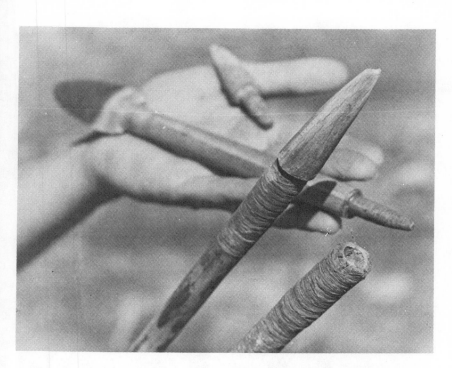

How I cut my foreshafts to fit the dart...this way isn't authentic and requires more care in fitting...but helps more in preventing splitting of the dart when you just might miss your target and hit something more solid. I use antler tips for general shooting. Stone tips would have been used for hunting.

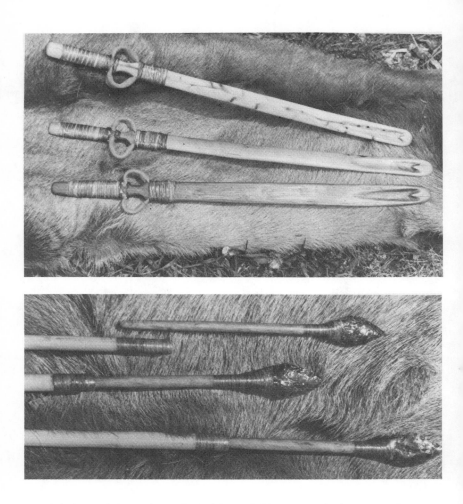

Atlatls and darts done the "old way". No counterbalance on the atlatls...foreshafts done the way that they were. These were done by my friend Jim Riggs of Oregon..who also took the photos.

INSECTS

Here...more so that with the other critters mentioned up to this point, you may have to really overcome prejudices. To go into any complete detail as to the edibility of various insects would require a book of it's own (Butterflies in my Stomach and Entertaining with Insects by Ronald L. Taylor are two good sources...unfortunately both are out of print but found in many libraries). I include here much useful information on the eating of many common insects...for more details and information on nutritional values I recommend the above books.

Grasshoppers/crickets/termites...all edible. Earthworms, yeah! Maggots too. MOST grubs. 'Bout any water insects. Caterpillars...GENERALLY. (Avoid the hairy ones...or any brightly colored ones...or any with any disagreeable odors.) In fact, the above rules of brightly colored and strong, disagreeable odors should be pretty much followed anywhere in nature. It's nature's way of warning off predators...including us!!

Wings and legs should be removed from most, such as the grasshoppers and crickets...not too good at digesting. I would cook any insect that I had my eye on eating. I have heard from some that this is unnecessary...but I still have that slight fear of parasites. Drying and grinding into a paste/flour and eaten this way or added to soups/stews is another way to include this nutrition into your diet. (Right now I am planning on my next book delving into the various methods of cooking under a primitive situation.) If worried about eating the contents of these critter's intestines, just impound them somewhere for a few hours and they will empty themselves out.

To help overcome your prejudice of eating insects, just remember that they eat leaves and grasses...do you know what chickens and hogs eat?...

MEAT PRESERVATION

Once you have stocked up on provisions, you also will need to know how to preserve some of your excess for the days that you have nothing...either for the long, late winter nights or for a journey. The simplest and easiest primitive method is simply to air dry it. Just about anything can be preserved by drying...even watermelon (though you might not have a hell of a lot left when done).

With this book, we're thinking mostly about meats. Jerky. What the aboriginals and early settlers used for trail foods and emergency food stores was known as jerked meat. This was simply meat, cut into thin strips (I've read that 1/4th of an inch or less thickness will keep the flies from blowing, laying eggs, on it), laid over racks and sun dried...or if the weather was wet, dried slowly in the smoke of the fire (which, by the way, was the only time that the early folks flavored their jerky...from the smoke...and that not intentionally). After a day or two or three, the meat was dried (jerked) and ready for storage, usually in rawhide containers to protect it from moisture. If kept dry, it would literally last forever. All the meat loses through this drying process is moisture. All nutrition remains...but remember, it has no fats. The jerky can be chewed as is (and chewed, and chewed, and chewed), or it can, and most often was, pounded and boiled and added to a stew, into which you an throw various roots, seeds, bugs...whatever.

In a more stable situation, other than overnight stops during a journey, the one step further, and a thousand times more valuable, method of preservation, is to make the jerked meat into pemmican. This is very simply pounding the dried meat, shredding it apart, and mixing it with fats. This is the ultimate in trail food. On it alone, one can live.

The suet, fats, of animals, is simmered, the impurities (scraps of meats, etc.) scraped or drained off. Here you want to be using animals such as deer, buffalo, beef. The resulting product is tallow (using pork, raccoon, bear, etc. leaves you lard...too soft). The prepared jerky is mixed with the tallow and you have the complete meal. This can, and was, kept in rawhide containers...all edges sealed with tallow (to insure that moisture was kept from the meat)...and it also is a forever preserved. Just be cautious to have the tallow "not hot" when mixing w/meat. <u>IF HOT, IT WILL COOK THE MEAT-WHICH CAN LEAD TO SPOILAGE AND POSSIBLE DEATH!</u> I like it just shy of setting up—still pourable. If set up too much, it will be difficult to completely cover/coat all the meat.

Venison strips and packrats drying in the sun

LEFT: Beef suet as taken from the critter...and diced to render.
RIGHT: Rendering. The mixture is cooked until completely
dissolved...strained...and then the remaining "junk" allowed to settle. The
result is clear (white when cooled) tallow.

LEFT: Pounding dried venison (jerky)...RIGHT: The resulting powder.
It could be added to stews as is.

LEFT: All the ingredients for "Wasna"...pemmican. Tallow/jerky/suet/ and rawhide envelope in which to put the finished product. RIGHT: Pouring tallow into the pounded jerky. BE CERTAIN THAT THE TALLOW HAS COOLED BEFORE MIXING WITH THE MEAT...OR YOU WILL COOK IT...<u>AND COOKED MEAT CAN AND WILL POISON YOU!</u>

LEFT: Finished mixing. I don't get too carried away with tallow...just enough to thoroughly coat the meat. RIGHT: Packing into rawhide envelope.

The filled envelope, packed with nourishment. It is nothing but dried meat mixed with some tallow. All that one needs to stay alive. The envelope sides (where it has been sewn with sinew) has also been dipped into the tallow to further protect the contents...and a layer of tallow has been poured over the top of the pemmican.

5

Primitive

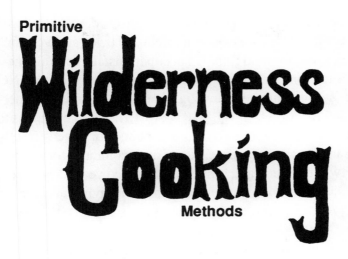

Methods

INTRODUCTION

What a year this last one has been ('88). We sure haven't spent any too much time here at home. I knew that there was <u>some</u> interest in primitive living, but I wasn't prepared for all the interest that I've found that the average American has along these lines.

What's the cause of this interest?

For me, (us), it's a freedom gained from reliance upon others..a freedom of dependency.

Every person living in this world, or even out of it (in a space capsule) is dependent upon the Earth for his/her existence. It don't matter who or where you are, the Earth supplies your wants and needs.

Geri's thought that everyone should be compelled to visit a slaughterhouse at least once during their growing years is a good one. It's mind-boggling just how many people think that everything just automatically comes pre-packaged.

Like it or not, we are a part <u>of</u> the Earth...not something separate from it. Face it...WE <u>ARE</u> ANIMALS. The only thing that differs us from other animals is the fact that we can reason...we are (supposedly) intelligent. (Here I had better slow it down a bit...I can get pretty worked up talking about

197

this.)

The folks that attend our workshops/demonstrations/ presentations/or whatever you might call it, are as diversified a bunch as one could find. All occupations/all races/all ages/ all educational levels/all (ALL?)...both sexes. There is NO ONE set of characteristics to define who is (or isn't) interested in from WHAT WE ALL CAME!!! It matters not as to what color/race you are. ALL of our ancestors lived directly with the Earth at one time...some are yet today...for some it was twenty years ago...others two hundred years. My ancestors were throwing sticks and stones and living in caves or huts just a scant few thousand years ago...along with most of yours.

No matter how "far we've come"...we are all yet tied to the Earth. What we wear...what we eat...what we live in...what we use for transportation...our phones...our (your) TV's and VCR's...the computers...EVERYTHING! It all derived from the Earth. It's just that we have evolved so far that in our society we are all specialists. We excel at one, or two, or three things...but beyond that limited knowledge someone else does everything for us. We are virtually slaves within our cultures.

If all man-made things quit at one time...the Earth wouldn't be bothered with the overpopulation of man anymore.

It seems that many are searching. Many realize the sad situation that we have gotten ourselves into...and many are trying to do at least a little bit about it. Just knowing these everyday living skills..just knowing...frees one from his dependency. When one is capable of going "Naked Into the Wilderness" and living pretty damn comfortably-very easily (under MOST situations this is no endurance test)...he is free. And the REAL satisfaction is undefinable. The look on ones' face as he/she blows up his/her first friction-made fire makes all the others who just kinda "push our button" worth the effort. I can't begin to explain the satisfaction in DOING

SOMETHING FOR YOURSELF...it would be about like trying to explain how in the American West the sky IS bigger...the distances ARE further. It can't really be explained. One has to experience for himself.

In the introduction of my second book, *Primitive Fire and Cordage,* (this is my fifth) I mentioned how the more one knows, the more that he realizes that he doesn't know. WOW...has this last year proved me right. Now that I have better than twenty thousand books in circulation, I receive more and more mail from readers...many of them who know a <u>whole lot</u>. There's a lot of knowledgeable folks out there..and many send me tips and ideas... Also during our travels we have come into contact with some of the nation's top experts in the various primitive skills fields...and what a joy to spend time with them. Now <u>I</u> get to sit back and learn. So many ways to get the same projects done.

Now, whenever I do use some others' ideas, I try to remember to credit him/her for it...so far I haven't forgotten anyone that I know of..BUT..what I have so far put forth to you, the reader, is MY way of doing things. (I say MY way...MY tanning method is actually the combination of tanning methods from several...I just picked and chose what, for me, was the easiest). What I do show in my books (and videos), is a WORKING method which YOU can apply. I have stated before..the way that I show is NOT THE ONLY WAY. But you now do have a WORKING book to guide you through to an end. What I show DOES work. I haven't copied from others what has been passed on as lore....without actually trying it out. If I say that it do work...IT DO!...(Remember there are usually several variations that can also be applied to any given situation). And if <u>I</u> can do it...YOU can.

It's all so easy.

As I have mentioned before...the price of this book...and all up to now...is three dollars. And it will stay that as long as the printer stays the same. I'm constantly given hell for not charging more. BUT...what we are trying to do thru our teachings is to educate...not make a million. Another way for me (us) to beat the system a little. I can't justify charging YOU seven or eight dollars for what costs me fifty cents (after first printing). At first I had difficulty in finding people to handle the books as there just isn't that much of a profit margin...(several, of course, did)...but now, because of YOU creating a demand for the books that WORK, dealers are calling me. For this I want to thank you.

Geri and I hope, for the most part, that thru our teachings that we might...just might...get through to one who may one day be in a position to make a decision that may affect our environment (chairman of the board of an oil company/a Senator or Congressman on a committee)...and that because of an increased awareness of nature...that one may make a RIGHT decision.

So, with this, the fifth book in my series to teach you to be able to go "Naked into the Wilderness", we will delve into various methods of cooking up some of the things that you've been shown how to catch...with no modern day pots and pans. We will hit several different methods of cooking something up...but remember...these are only some of the methods that will work. There are certainly several...

Don't limit your learning to only this series. I want to constantly stress that others do things their way..and it also works. And use your own head...imagination..that thing that most threw away after childhood..and experiment for yourself. You're getting a good base from which to work.

Oct. 1988

COOK: to prepare food for eating by heating.

Simple...yeah, really.

For most people of today, you take away their pots, pans, skillets and there would be a problem. But, like any of the other primitive living skills, once you think about it (or have it shown to you), it really is easy.

IN THE COALS

Most boys of the outdoors, at least in my day, didn't concern themselves with a lot of extra "junk" to carry around. Travel light was the thing. Wieners, potatoes and corn on the

The daily special...at least that
day's...field mouse.

cob thrown directly into the coals...sticks to move them around and get them out when ready (and also to scrape off some of the excess ashes). (We also sometimes carried a can of beans or stew and almost always a small pan to heat water, or melt snow, for coffee or hot chocolate...remember, Dave?).

So. To throw your meal directly into the coals <u>is</u> the easiest way to cook up something. A little bit of ashes won't hurt a body..but remember that ashes make lye...and lye will eat <u>you</u>. So, for safety sake, a little ashes should go a long way.

Jim Riggs of Oregon, with his students, just singes the hair off deer mice over flames and throws them directly into the coals until done "just right"...crispy...and not too mushy on the inside. Nothing wasted here. They eat the whole thing...a good way to pick up extra vitamins.

After singeing hair off and roasting in coals.

Geri's first bite.

"Can I swallow now?"...really awfully dry (overdone?).

If it didn't kill her (and Jim and Marie and whom-
ever), I guess that it won't kill me. Remember, this
is all mouse...no gutting or skinning.

Packing small game and birds in a mud/clay pack works
well also. Not just any "mud" will work...it needs to be
somewhat sticky so that it doesn't crumble apart on you. Get

Trout being wrapped in clay/mud.

Sealed mudded trout.

the pack as airtight as possible so as to keep all juices in. This method has a coupla advantages. You don't need to skin/ singe/pluck the game..it all will stick to the mud and fall away from the meat. You can also pack tubers and veggies

Laid on coals. More raked onto this. (note oven at far right)

all in the same package. Gutting it is your choice. In a real primitive or survival situation you may elect to eat it all to get all the nourishment that is available.

Finished. The mud/clay pulls away the skin (feathers and skins of birds) and you are left with tasty trout...done just right. You'll hafta kinda guess the time depending on the coals. This was about twenty minutes.

Have you ever cooked corn on the cob directly on the coals at a barbecue? Just dip the ear in water and it will steam as it cooks. The same can be done with other edibles, though be a bit choosy when you pick the greenery to wrap the food in as flavors will be added to the food. Certain leaves (oak/walnut) can leave a bitter taste. Certainly avoid poison ivy/oak/sumac, etc. And a little sage goes a long way. Sometimes grasses plaited together, or cattail leaves, green and/or wetted will help protect the outside from burning and also kinda steam the meal.

Ash cake placed in coals.

If you have any type of flour, make a dough by mixing w/ water. Pat the dough thicker for doughy/thinner for crispy. Throw into the ashes and you have "ash cakes".

BROIL

What a romantic scene. A deer/rabbit/bird skewered onto a stick that is placed onto two forked sticks and supported over the fire.

But, when you turn the stick, the critter stays in the same position, not turning with the stick.

How often I've seen that. It is a great way to cook. But too often I've seen those who don't know how to keep the meat turning with the stick.

One simple way. Poke a hole (or two) through the <u>green</u> stick which skewers the animal. Then run another stick through the animal, the stick, and back out thru the animal again. If you don't have a knife, a sharp, pointed rock or dead sharp piece of wood, preferably hardwood, should split the green skewer easily enough. With this method you can cook anything from a mouse to a buffalo.

Cornish hen and trout laid out to be spitted. Note holes in skewers and aligned pins.

208

Hen and trout cooking. Since fire was built on solid rock we couldn't use sticks as uprights to hold skewers...so rocks were utilized. Rocks on skewers are to keep the meals from rotating and falling to lowest balance.

Again, if flour is available, wrap your dough directly onto a stick and prop it over the coals.

A steak, roast, fish or bird can also be stuck onto a green stick and pinned as above...or use two sticks at angles...and prop it over the fire/coals. Turn as necessary.

Another trick (from Harry from Troy, Montana). Fold two thin, pliable saplings back on themselves and place your fish, or whatever, inside and hold or prop over the fire/coals.

The cooking methods that we've covered up to now, most would get figured out pretty quick if necessity arose. Some, not all, of what we hit now will be things that are not so often or easily figured out by many.

Overall view of "working" fire.

Close up of frying potatoes and grasshoppers.

Getting kinda crowded. Ash cake in coals
(upper), dough on stick (upper right)
venison steak on sticks (center) and
potatoes and grasshoppers frying on flat
rock top of oven (lower).

A lot of food from one fire. One normally wouldn't cook all methods at once...but for photos? Top is baked (mud) fish. Right of that is broiled steak. Center is hen and trout rotisseried. Left of that is trout and potato baked in oven. Lower left is ash cake and bread baked on stick. To the right of that is fried potatoes/grasshoppers. To the extreme right, the gourmets' delight, roasted mouse.

BAKING

Not cakes and pies. Just the same old stuff that we've been cooking up till now. But, by making an oven (of sorts) we are freed of watching quite so carefully what's going on so as not to burn supper.

About any time that we build a cooking fire, at one end we build a small oven of rocks...as flat as we can get them, but on occasion flat rocks are not available...careful choosing/banging/placing of round rocks will make a serviceable oven (of sorts).

The fire is built. As it burns down, coals are raked into and around and over the oven. Heat the rocks slowly so that any water that may be inside the stone has a chance to leave...slowly. Heat too fast and the steam may leave too fast...as in BANG!

We usually build a longish fire (pit?), Active burning at one end...coals in the middle...oven at the other end. Our ovens are normally only three to four inches high and deep by about six inches wide, only larger if necessary. Smaller ovens are more efficient for small things...pieces of meat/potatoes/tubers/veggies/birds/dough for a bread of sorts. We keep coals in front and on top (and sides if it works out, but not all that necessary)...and foods are done just as quick as in the oven at home.

Another easy oven. Dig into the base of a bank (dirt bank). If it happens to be clay, fine. If not, line with flat rocks. Build your fire inside and let heat. When ready, just scrape out and keep coals/fire at or near the entrance.

Now, in conjunction with the first of these ovens, you have right at hand a frying pan...your hot, flat rock that makes the top of the oven. You can fry about anything here that you can at home (maybe not over-easy eggs without lots of practice...and luck!)

One other oven "type" way to cook is also a hole in the ground. Dig a hole plenty large enough for what you intend to place in it. You'll want some extra space. (note photos) There are many, many variations to this "pit" cooking. You just pick and choose what works for you.

If the soil is clay-like, fire it by building a hot fire within. If the soil is sandy or crumbly, line it with flat stones.

Build a fire in the prepared hole. I prefer to leave the coals in the hole. I put a handful of green sticks/twigs directly onto the coals...followed by a layer of green/wetted grass...maybe some cattail leaves (green) if available...and then the meal. The green sticks/twigs will add a great smoke flavoring. The wet/green grasses and cattail leaves add moisture and also protect the meal from direct contact with the coals. Do remember though, the particular tastes of the leaves/grasses, etc. will also stay with the meal.

Then in goes the meal. Meat/roots/nuts/whatever.

Cover the hole with a flat rock that has been preheated and seal. Place coals on the rock. Now the food is heated from above and below...but more of a steam heat. Trial and error will dictate the time. Because of the moist heat, you really can't overcook. Figure three to five hours for most "average" sized meals.

The fact that oxygen can't fuel the fire will keep the thing from bursting into flames—the importance of covering coals and sealing the hole as fast as possible.

If a flat rock is not available...build a supporting layer of sticks at the top of the pit and cover it with a jacket/shirt/blanket/grasses (grasses not the best because this will leak some dirt). Then proceed to seal this with plenty of dirt. This will also work better if the dirt has been preheated by building a fire over it. Because the pit is sealed <u>air-tight</u>, and by taking particular care to cover the coals with moist greenery, no flames <u>should</u> appear.

Now you have several hours to forage/trap/build without having to tend your meal.

(L) Rock lid being heated...(R) All laid out...chicken and potatoes, (lower) green sticks (middle) and wet grasses and green and wetted cattail leaves.

(L) Green sticks placed directly onto coals (to keep grasses from coming in direct contact). Also note rocks lining the hole which helps to retain heat. (R) Placing grasses and cattail leaves in hole.

(L) Now in goes the meal and (R) laying the rock lid and sealing ALL openings first w/grasses and then dirt. You want it sealed until no smoke is seen escaping. If air enters the meal can be burned. We also piled about six inches of dirt on top to help keep in the heat. Since the rock was already hot clear thru we didn't build a fire on top...which can be done.

The finished meal. Here we let it cook for only 2 1/2 hours because of failing daylight (need for photo's). Chicken was perfect...just beginning to fall from the bones. The potatoes done, but firm.

BOILING

One of the best reasons that I know of for knowing how to boil something in a primitive situation (and there are several), is to make a little bit go a long way. One smallish piece of meat (rat/squirrel/coupla mice, bird, even fish)boiled will help to fill one's (or more) belly faster than just eating the critter. And to the broth can be added any number of other nutritious things that one has gathered during the day (seeds/nuts/insects/edible plants). And though it's not the thing that one would normally be able to accomplish on one's first night in a primitive situation, unless awfully lucky to find just the right "pot", it also isn't difficult to come across a "pot".

What we're gonna do in this situation is to heat the water using hot rocks...called, appropriately, hot rock cooking.

Though most rocks will do the job, one does need to be somewhat selective. Some will just crumble (sandstones) and others can, and do, explode (flints/cherts/obsidian). YOU will need to do the checking if you can't tell the difference. And do be aware of the danger of exploding rocks. I ASSUME NO RESPONSIBILITY FOR ANY INJURY RESULTING FROM EXPLODING ROCKS...But just a bit of knowledge and common sense will prevent any (or most) mishaps.

I generally prefer "creek rocks", NOT FOUND IN CREEKS. The hard, roundish granite type stones seem to me to work about the best. Just pick them from higher ground. Those that have been soaked in water just might have gotten moisture inside thru tiny cracks which, when heated, can't get out slowly enough for the crack to accommodate...and so, bang.

We have used softer limestone and pumice...both heat well but eventually (as do all rocks that I've used) break apart. These softer ones also have the tendency to leave a grit in the soup/stew...though that may help to keep your insides reamed out.

Heat the rocks. It's best to build a good solid foundation of wood on which to build your fire...as all rocks eventually fall into the deepest part of the fire...which may not be the hottest if it happens to be just the ground. Layer wood and rocks. We generally use about a dozen rocks to heat a gallon+/- of water...and the temperature of the water is usually awfully cold. As the first rocks are taken from the water as they cool, place them in a section of "new" fire...when you run outta rocks the first time thru and you're not done cooking, the first ones used will have heated again and be ready to go. The second section of fire also helps to distinguish which rocks are which.

The pot. We have always used a fresh deer skin for our pot. Either set into a hole in the ground and staked around, or tied into a tripod of sticks. Usually the hair is left on. We generally cook this way when demonstrating brain tanning and use the freshly fleshed (say that ten times fast) skin...hair side out, of course. You need not even flesh the skin...the flesh and fats adding to the meal. The skin will shrink considerably as it also cooks...so take this into account or you'll have broth all over the place. We normally leave lots of slack in the skin when cooking in a hole. Tied to a tripod, it'll just shrink...so don't fill it as full. You'll hafta kinda just feel this out.

A larger animal's stomach can, and has been, used also and here you have the added advantage of being able to eat the pot.

A depression large enough in a rock would be great...as long as it's convenient for/to camp.

A solid piece of wood will work fine also...though it will take some time to hollow it out (easiest with fire). In a semi-permanent camp, this would be no problem.

A clay pot is the cat's meow. Though this could also be

just placed into the fire (I plan to have a book devoted to primitive pottery as part of this series).

A tightly coiled basket will work. I've always thought that they needed to be lined with pitch but have been told otherwise by those who should know. Almost had one to cook in this summer, but the "pot" got tied up and couldn't make it.

A hole dug in the ground (ground that wouldn't leak) would surely work. So much the better if the ground happened to be clayish...build a fire in it first and you have a non-moveable pot.

Now, let's get cooking.

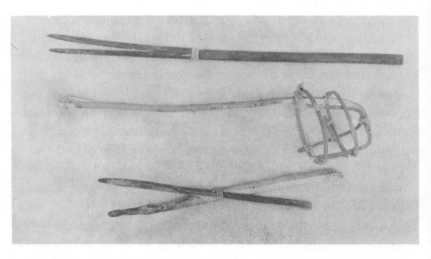

Tools handy for hot rock cooking. Two types of "tongs" (top and bottom) and a basket to hold the rocks while immersing into the skin pot...saves wear and tear on the pot when taking rocks out. Simple forked sticks can be used in lieu of tongs.

When we first started hot rock cooking, we just used forked sticks and placed the hot rocks directly into the skin pot. Being careful removing the rocks from the pot we were able to get two or three meals out of one skin...then finally a hole would appear in the weakened skin and supper (the broth anyhow) literally went down the drain. We now make a small basket/carrier for to put the rocks into and then place that in the pot. MUCH easier on the pot. You can sometimes place three or four rocks into the carrier. It's best to have the carrier in the soup before putting the hot rocks in as they have a tendency to burn thru the cordage holding it together...the rocks being red hot, or near to it. The photos will show the tools we normally use...but remember, just forked sticks will do.

I know that cooked meat can poison you if it spoils-since

Everything gathered and ready for boiling. Hole dug...deer skin and stakes...rocks and wood...and rocks and wood layered ready to be fired.

221

the rawhide pot does cook, I don't know how to judge this - common sense should dictate here - don't let the "cooked" pot get too old.

It normally takes from five to ten fist-sized rocks, red hot, to bring the water to a boil. Remember, this is usually mountain creek water...mighty cold! Figure about ten minutes or less. Once boiling, it only takes one or two rocks in the basket at a time to keep the brew simmering for three to five minutes. When first placed in the brew it will boil like a hot springs, and then settle down to a simmer. You can hear the rock(s) cooking/sizzling. When it slows down, take it/them out and replace with new. You will be cooking as fast as you would on a stove. In fact, the water will boil hotter at higher elevations and so cook faster. I know of one fellow who does

Skin staked out and filled with water. Skin will shrink considerably while boiling so extra slack is left in hole. Rocks heating in background.

all of his camp boiling with hot rocks (in a dutch oven) while in the mountains just because it does cook faster. And if you saw the size of this guy, you'd know why he wanted/needed his food faster.

When rocks have heated, the fire is stretched out so that when cool rocks are removed from the vat they can be reheated...also keeping the two batches of rocks separate.

Using "tongs" to place hot rocks into basket...in the water to help keep burning thru the basket.

Rocks...in basket...in broth.

After several rocks (in this case about ten) the water comes immediately to a rolling boil upon immersion and will simmer for from three to five minutes.

I'll touch on one other method for to (kinda) boil.

We have for quite sometime used dehaired deer rawhide for water buckets.

I've seen water boiled in a paper cup placed directly in a fire.

Take note that paper and deer rawhide are not the same.

The pot/bucket at first will leak readily. After some soaking (a few to several hours) it somehow seals itself. One bucket that we've carried for over a year and always fill with

Rawhide bucket directly over the coals. It
works...but. If no rocks were available this would be
a good second choice...though ruining a good skin.

226

water at workshops/demos "leaks" not at all...though water does filter through and evaporate...thereby keeping the contents cool.

Well, we carried all summer a pot of deer rawhide, a nice skin too, with the intention of cooking in it. We did.

First...lots of coals and little flame. Our pot is held together by natural fiber cordage and several times flames were licking close. It was a hassle.

And the skin kept springing leaks (dripping). No rhyme or reason. Just when and wherever they felt like it. And then they'd quit. Not enough to put the fire out (just drips)..but a real pain. It kept the fire cool. We worked for about two hours and never did get the damn thing to "BOIL". It did simmer, and would have cooked after the first 15 or 20 minutes or so. But boil...no.

It also shrank to almost half it's original size. We had to constantly dip water out.

Hot rocks...much more effective and faster.

Water dripping from rawhide pot.

6

DEER
from

Field
to
Freezer

INTRODUCTION

March 1989

So, now you've shot your deer. What next!?

The quality of wild game (or even domesticated) meats begins right here.

The first thing that one has to do is to remove the insides. The longer that these remain in the carcass, the more chance that there is for spoilage. Once a critter dies it immediately begins to spoil...we have to stop this action if we want the meat to taste anything like decent.

If properly shot in the first place (head/neck/chest cavity), the removal of the insides is a fairly clean job. With a gut shot animal, the procedures shown still apply but the job just won't be as pleasant.

Removal of the ---we'll use the word guts here--- not only keeps any extra adverse tastes from entering the meat but more importantly it BEGINS COOLING THE CARCASS which will stop, or at least slow down, the decaying process---temporarily. Cooling of the carcass is my first action. I do this by immediately field dressing the game. Then, especially if the weather is warm, by removing the skin from the animal. With deer, this is especially important as their hollow hair acts as an insulation which keeps the heat from leaving the carcass. About the only time that I refrain from immediately removing the skin is when the temperature is well below freezing and I really don't want the carcass to freeze.

Some people "hang" their animal for periods ranging from a few days for up to two weeks. We do if the weather permits. I feel that hanging has nothing to do with the taste of the meat but what happens is that the meat fibers are allowed to "relax"---somewhat acting as a tenderizer--- especially good for big old bucks. But for this to be successful, the temperature needs to be approximately 38 to 40 degrees. If warmer, the meat will begin to rot---if frozen it will do no good.

Most all people will have with them a knife of sorts---in fact many people have with them TOO much knife. A deer can be field dressed/skinned and cut up using nothing more than a fingernail file. We will illustrate here the entire process using not a fingernail file, but a few stone blades that we knocked from a piece of local chert---doing this to show that if we can do the complete process using nothing but a piece of stone---you certainly can do it using any or all modern day tools available to you.

The basic principles shown here can also apply to just about any other animal...from squirrel to buffalo.

FIELD DRESSING

Here we have a nice doe---shot not more than a few minutes back---in the chest. If possible, I like to place the animal so that it's on an incline, head down, so that the guts are pushed by gravity out of the way while I work. Note that the hind legs have already been partially skinned for attachment of the tag through the hind tendons. Laid out are several stone blades...the round rocks are for re-sharpening if necessary. The bone knives we never did use...but they would have also worked.

Our purpose now is to open the animal from one end to the other...from the anus to the throat---and remove all that lies in between. You'll soon see that it's all attached and "pulling the cord" from either end will remove it all. Here, we'll pull from the throat back but just the reverse will do as well.

Place rocks or sticks on either side of the animal to keep it lying upright.

These photos show making the first incision...carefully pulling the skin out so as not to cut through the stomach lining

After having cut through the skin for about six to eight inches up from the anus, we have cut here through the meat down to the pelvic bone. You can readily feel the pointed ridge of the pelvis...which we'll split to free the bowel. Here some people take a long bladed "sharp" knife and reach thru the anal opening and make a circular cut to free this. I have always found splitting the bone much easier. We here illustrate using a sharp edged rock to do the splitting...a

regular hunting knife will make this much easier. When splitting the bone, force the legs apart and with just a slight tap of some sort of hammer, on most deer, it will seem to fall apart---but you have to cut in exactly the right spot...on top of the ridge where you can "feel" where the bone is "welded" together..otherwise you'll be "cutting" and not "splitting". You will also need to cut just slightly through the stomach membrane right above the pelvis to relieve the tension preventing you from forcing it apart....be careful not to cut through the innards.

Many accounts have you tying off the end of the bowel. We just don't mess with this. If careful, nothing will spill out...and if it does it is nothing but firm pellets that won't have a tendency to contaminate. You do as you wish.

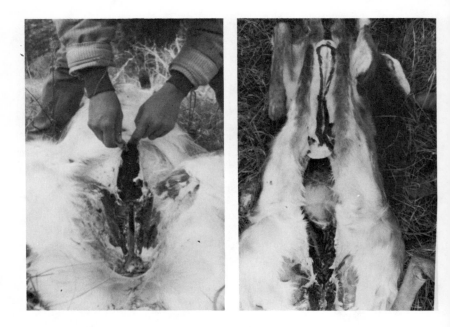

Once this delicate task has been taken care of, cut carefully all the way to the throat. If the animal is placed on an incline as noted earlier, the guts will not have a tendency to spill out...there-by getting in your way. If an incline just ain't there, place wood/rocks/whatever under the hind end. You do want to be careful not to cut into the innards. Normally I will first split the skin...then open the stomach cavity.

You won't be able to open the sternum (breastbone) by just slicing. With a steel knife you need just stand over the animal, facing it's head, and thrust upward. All,except the biggest and oldest of animals will split this way. Illustrated here we split with a sharp edged stone...hammering with a wooden club. Then cut the animals throat to free the windpipe. (I don't bleed my game. Once a deer is dead, it's heart stops beating and the blood stops flowing...unlike a pig which will spurt blood for many minutes).

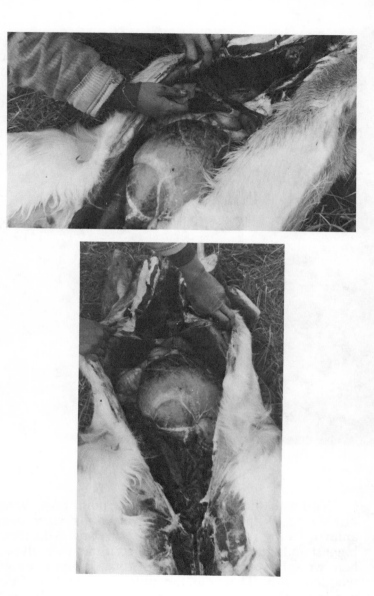

Now, before we begin to take it apart, we need to cut out the diaphragm...which separates the chest and stomach cavities. Just cut it free from the walls...no big deal.

NOW...we're ready to pull it all out. As mentioned before, you can pull from either end. Here we show pulling with the windpipe...using the knife for most of the way to free it from along the backbone. At this stage it's easier to turn the animal sideways on the incline. With very little effort the guts will fall out.

238

If there is snow on the ground, I'll now turn the animal over and let it drain and also cool. Unless the animal has been shot in the guts, the inside of the carcass will be as clean as it should be...though if snow is not available, I will rinse with cold water first chance I get to help cool it if the temp. is up.

The animal is now field dressed.

SKINNING

Skinning the animal is the next chore. I was first taught to skin deer while it laid on the ground...and it does work well. The main problem with this is that it seems to require more knife use than I like. First split the legs to the center line and then push/pull/fist/cut the skin off...first one side to the backbone and then roll the animal over onto the skin already loosened and repeat on the other side. Real tough on backs also.

I hang most all of the deer that I skin from the hind legs, kept spread apart with a stick, after having first split the skin of the legs up the center to the already split belly.

After these initial opening cuts, the knife can be put aside. By pulling and fisting (pulling the skin with one hand while pushing the fist of the other between skin and carcass), the skin will separate readily from the carcass...especially if the critter is still warm.

(L)Pulling skin from hams and (R) pulling over tail.

240

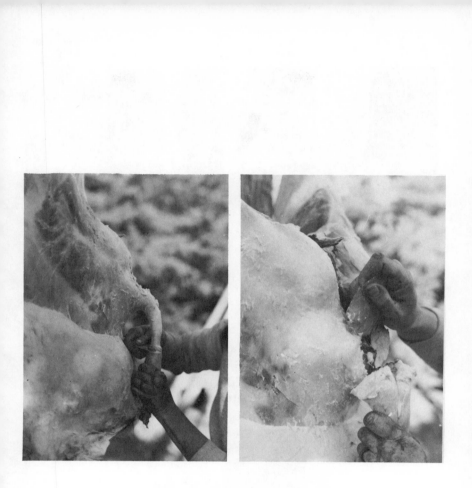

(L) Cutting skin from tail...(I almost never leave the tail on the skin for tanning)...(R) Cutting the tail loose from the body .

Both photo's showing fisting skin off. A bit extra care is taken around the front shoulder (R) as here the layers of meat/membrane tend to overlap.

Pulling skin from front legs.

Deer parted from it's coat.

REMOVING HEAD

No saw is needed in any of this. Removing the head is simple. Find where the head swivels, where the neck and head meet---cut through the meat to the bone.

Twist and snap...

and cut loose remaining membrane/tendons.

CUTTING OFF OF LEGS

Here I'm gonna show you a simple method of removing the legs...shown to me by an old butcher friend of mine (Argel Pultz of Riley, Ks.). You need actually only follow the series of photo's as they are pretty self explanatory.

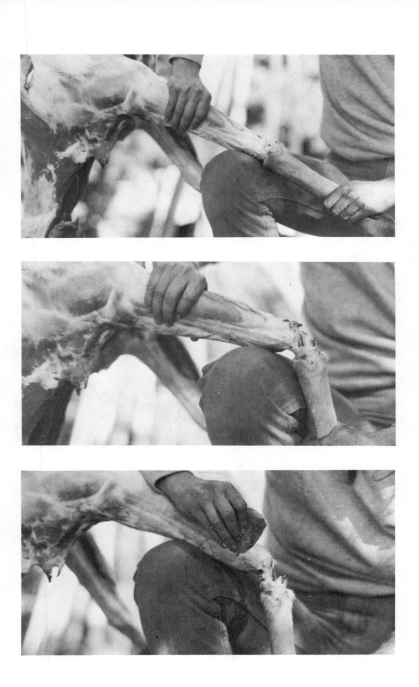

SINEW REMOVAL

If you're following and/or practicing primitive skills at all, you will want to save the sinew...there are many, many uses for this as explained in several of my other booklets.

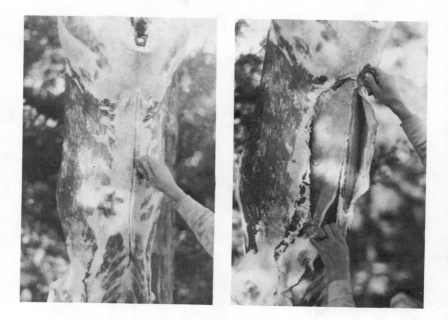

(L) cutting through outer layer of fat next to backbone...both sides. (R) Pulling away layer of fat exposing sinew as shiny silver membrane (tendon) covering loins.

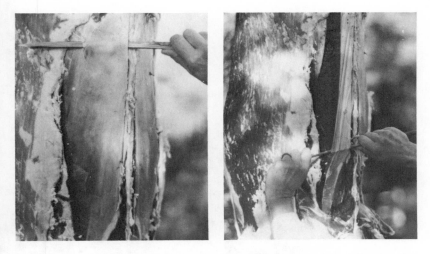

(L) putting stick (dull knife is what we generally use) between sinew and loin meat and (R) pulling down with a smooth motion while jiggling the stick to separate sinew cleanly from the loin

(L) Using stick to clean strip as much as possible before removal. (R) Pushing fingers down following sinew strip to separate it from meats...both sides.

(L) A slight tug will pull free the strip at the shoulder (cutting it here looses two to three inches) and (R) cutting free at the hip where the sinew draws into a cord.

REMOVING LOIN AND TENDERLOIN

The bestest of the best. Loins and/or tenderloins, cut into butterfly steaks.

After removing the sinew, the loins are what lies underneath. Removing (L) is simple...a knife is hardly needed...they can simply be pulled loose (though a knife makes a neater job of it). The tenderloin is the smaller strip of meat lying against the backbone on the inside (R)...this also can be pulled loose, though again a knife makes it neater.

One each of the strips showing relative size.

Cutting into thick steaks

Cutting these again to make them "butterflies".

Butterflies cut from one each loin and tenderloin.

CUTTING UP OF CARCASS

Removing front shoulder...knife will find it's own way.

Separating side meat from hind quarters.

Cutting away hind quarter...again blade will find it's own way.

Pieces...and cutter...all laid out.

MEAT CUTTING

We bone all our meat and that's what we'll show here.

Geri with HIND QUARTER.

Hind quarter laid out w/first two cuts made.

All meat separated from bones.

Hind quarter...bone...steaks and roasts.

Geri with FRONT SHOULDER.

Boned.

Front shoulder bone...roasts and stew meat.

Geri with MAIN BODY.

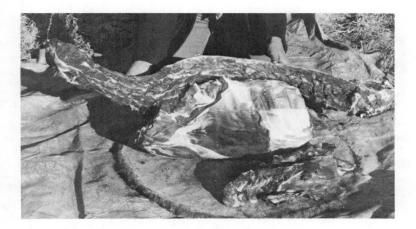

Excess meats removed...for ham (deer) burger or (for us) stew.

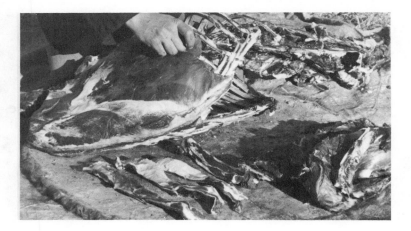

Cutting meat from ribs. We prepare boneless ribs and enjoy them thoroughly...meat from here could also be used as stew or deerburger.

Clean carcass...pile of rib meat and meat for stew or burger.

And that, folks, is all there is to it. REALLY very simple. We don't begin to pretend that we're butchers...far from it. BUT...as Geri say's...all that really matters is to get the meat small emough to fit into a frying pan.

Go to it!

7

Primitive Wilderness

Containers

Book 1
BASKETS/BAGS & WHAT-NOTS

INTRODUCTION
August 1989

Containers. No hunter/gatherer is worth his/her salt without something into which to put their gatherings.

As in most other aspects of primitive living, putting together a suitable container is in actuality much easier than one first suspects ... especially with the cumulative knowledge that the reader/student has gained in some of the other aspects of primitive living that have been covered thus far in our series. And the importance of some suitable container can't be stressed enough ... it really do make life easier. Remember ... "Naked into the Wilderness" ... and you ain't got no pockets.

What you will encounter here-in will be a lot of photos with some descriptive words ... I figure that the photos pretty well speak for themselves. This is far from the final word on containers ... what you will encounter here are several that have worked for us ... FUNCTIONAL ... no artwork. There are many, many ideas that will work as well ... much that we haven't covered ... not only due to lack of space but also due to the lack of knowledge. We do show workable products ... and most importantly explain the characteristics that one needs to look for in order to get the job done in his/her region.

This is a series of books ... which didn't begin that way at all ... gaining momentum and direction as it went along. I THINK that now I can safely list what the remaining books will be, and barring any great catastrophic events, I do expect the completion of the series late in 1990 or mid 1991 at the latest. As stressed before; the books will complete a circle ... enabling one to actually go "Naked into the Wilderness".

#8	CONTAINERS - BOOK 2, Primitive Pottery
#9	SEMI-PERMANENT SHELTERS
#10	TOOL MAKING, mostly basic flintknapping but also to include shell, bone, wood, etc.
#11	the USE OF THESE TOOLS to complete the projects shown thus-far in the series.
#12	if necessary, and probably so, to include any FURTHER TIPS/IDEAS that tie in with primitive living.

So, with that - lets get on with the subject at hand.

BASKETS

The first container that would come to mind to most would be a basket. Here we are going to show you three methods to obtain this. And do remember that this will be far from a definitive answer to your questions on basketry...but these are three methods that will work well to give you a finished product. And you need not stick to just any one of these methods...you can mix and match as you will. And to all of you artists in basketry out there...please bear with us and remember that these are FUNCTIONAL.

MATERIALS

As will be shown, many things in nature will work well in basketry. One need only search out particular characteristics....mainly that it is, or can be made to be, pliable. And it do help if it will remain somewhat so after the project has been completed so that it won't fall apart in use.....tho the purpose of the basket will help to dictate this---if to be used only for gathering nuts (the ones growing on trees, not those living in them)/herbs, etc., a lighter duty basket will suffice. If gathering heavy duty rocks or whatever (and remember, us cavemen do need our rocks), then a brittle basket will be wasted. The longer that the material is, the less splicing in is necessary.

Stick baskets, as I refer to those made of sticks, can, and should be made more pliable thru soaking for several hours/days, depending upon the material (dogwood and willow being what we predominantly use).....you can use this as a guide, but DO search out your area to find what it has to offer. And, as you will see, many other materials can and are used---cattails/any cordage/some barks/grass. As we approach these various materials here-in, we'll explain it's preparation.

WARPS, WEFTS AND WOOFS

These are what your baskets are comprised of. Warps are the longitudal threads/sticks/cords into which the wefts (also known as woofs) are threaded....a simple definition --- sometimes not quite so simply accomplished.

TWINING

In twining you are working with two wefts, normally twisting these once, between warps.

266

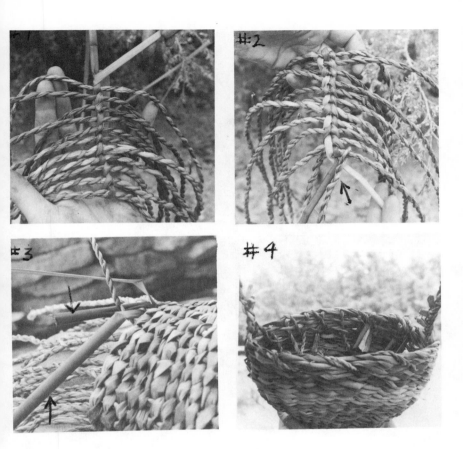

With this basket (actually here a bag) shown in the process of making, we are utilizing cattails exclusively as the material. These were cut dead in winter and allowed to dry (remember, cattails grow where it's wet), and resoaked --- then corded for the warps, cording allowing for a stronger basket/bag. (Cording is taught in detail in book #2). Then a single piece of cattail, wet, was twined in. Note in photo #2 that an additional warp has been added (lower center, arrow). As we proceed, you will find that warps will be added as necessary for strength. In photo #3, note the splicing in of a new weft....the upper arrow showing the last of the old, the lower arrow pointing to the new. Photo #4 shows, on the far side, how the warps have been threaded down into the wefts to finish. Another cord has been wrapped around the perimeter for added strength.

This bag, also twined, has been made from a variety of materials. Elm bark was corded for the warps and the bottom coupla inches was single strand elm bark---followed by a few inches of Western dogbane---this followed by several more inches of Eastern dogbane (not corded---the fibers only cleaned and then twined in)---finishing the top several inches with grass...(what we call slough grass ((grows in wet areas)), others have called it canary reed grass. We don't know what it is...but it do work. We found it following the guidelines pointed out earlier....something pliable and long enough to work with). The strap is brain tanned deer skin (book #1).

This burden basket, appropriately named, is made mostly from dogwood with a bit of willow tossed in. Deer rawhide supports the basket to which is tied a tumpline of brain tan...the tumpline to go around the shoulders or the head when carrying, leaving the hands free.

BASKET WEAVE

---is, of course, to weave a basket.

There are many ways in which you can begin your warps (your up and downers)---and this step is almost always the most difficult. One seems to never have near enough hands for this...sticks are always wanting to fall apart here...just persevere and it'll work.

Now, when basket weaving, you need to have an ODD number of warps for the weaving to work out. With twining it makes no difference.

So here note, in photo #1, the addition of a 13th warp in the upper left. Here Geri, she did most all the basket work illustrated, simply laid three shoots (willow) on three others (making for 12 warps) ...and made several wraps using the basket weave, which is simply one over and the next under the warp....she then stuck another shoot in, in order to make an odd number, and from here out the basket weave achieves it's purpose, alternating one above and one below on each full turn. After only a few wraps she decided to bend the shoots upwards in order to make for more of a cylindrical basket.

Photo #5 illustrates how warps are added in as we go.

Now, in photo's #6 &7 we show how to bend the ends of the shoots over and shove them into the space provided next to the next warp....got that? Naturally, cut them just a coupla inches long for this.

Photo #8 is the finished basket...#9 with the addition of a cordage strap.

Now here, we have quite a combination. Using willow, photo #1, we begin with the basket weave---changing to a twining in photo #2. #3 just

shows the same from the side. In photo #4 we have the basket completed--- using slough grass, wetted, in a basket weave the rest of the way. A surprising useful basket and much stronger than one would expect.

In these two photos, a side and a bottom view, we see a different variation of twining---very useful in baskets that can use spacing, such as fish traps. This was made for and sent to us by a master basket maker friend of ours in California who wishes to remain anonymous.

COILED BASKET

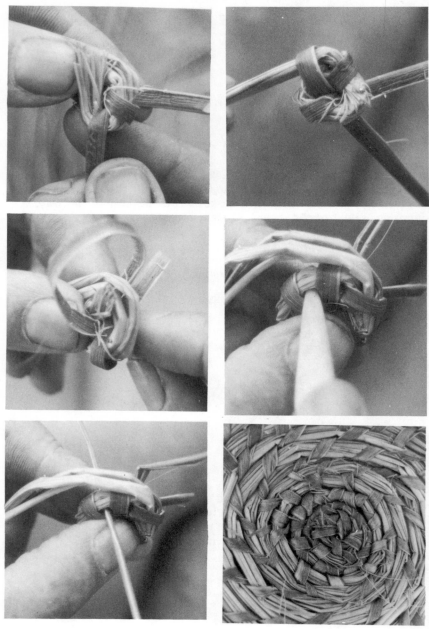

In the photos on the preceding page, you will have to study closely all the photos...remembering that starting is the hardest part of all. We are using here only slough grass and tying it together with yucca...though most any cordage type material would suffice. The middle photo on the right shows Geri opening a passageway for the yucca using a bone awl.

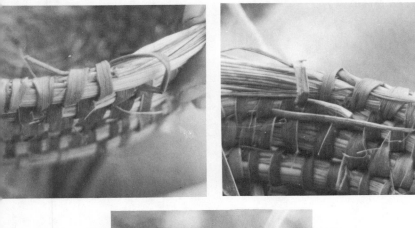

The next three photos show (top left) ending off a piece of yucca and bringing it under the preceding two loops. (top right) From the inside of basket at same tie off, beginning with a new strand and (bottom) showing from the outside beginning anew after the initial tie-in.

The last series shows how to tie off/finish the basket. The bottom right photo showing flint blade to be used in cutting off loose ends.

The finished basket.

BARK CONTAINER

Bark can be used in a surprisingly number of ways in the field...one concerning us here is the making of containers. And this also is one of the quickest means of ending with a finished container. What we illustrate in the photos is working with red cedar, Eastern or Western, I can't get a straight answer, though for our purposes I don't think that it really matters--- remember, what we are looking for is the characteristics. First priority is that it easily separate from the tree...also that when it dries that it won't be so fragile and brittle that it will self destruct. Most all of us know that birch bark works for any number of containers, including the famous canoe. The first "other" bark container that I was presented with was made of juniper (one of which is illustrated later). Another is the tulip poplar. Experiment around.

Since the photos are self explanatory, I'll list here the more important aspects to be aware of. You'll note that any holes are drilled into the bark...not cut. The bark really wants to split so care must be taken. When the container is finished, place it over an object that it will force it to keep it's shape as it dries. Here we used a log. Also note that in the two photos where I tie the container together, each is done differently. One uses a series of holes with cordage run through in such a way that there is a hole for the cord to run thru...and also that the cord runs around the container. In the other, only one tie at the top...the rest held together only with the cord. The pointed sides of the bottoms makes it easy to tie the cordage off there adding more strength.

The two bark containers on the left were made by and given to us by our friends Ken and Lynn Berry of Alabama, using tulip poplar. Note the wooden handle on the one on the left and also how they are tied. The one on the right was made from juniper (some species of cedar I think---ever heard of a juniper chest?)---is tied together with brain tan...makes a fine quiver. Made by friend Brian James of Washington state.

CORDAGE

Cordage is covered in depth in book #2 and we won't go into it again here...except to note, that, although not necessarily a "container", cordage can sure haul a lot of stuff on a gathering expedition...and it can also be made on the spot in many circumstances. Note here a variety of cordage made from natural materials (L) and also the general carryall utilizing it (R).

STONE

Some stones are soft enough to work with. The accompanying photos show soapstone just beginning to be worked (1), working materials of bone/antler/sharp cutting stones and a hammerstone (2). #3 shows Geri hard at it and #4 the finished product. This material works super easy and was used extensively in days of old where it was available...BUT BEWARE... SOAPSTONE, AT LEAST SOME OF IT, DO CONTAIN ASBESTOS WHICH CAN BE HARMFUL TO YOUR HEALTH.

We have used limestone (our limestone...not what is found in the S.E.), and though it can be used for hot rock cooking, it will not withstand the higher temperatures of placing it directly into the fire.

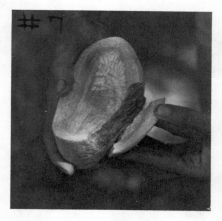

Photo #5 shows a beautiful soapstone bowl, a gift from Steve Watts of Gastonia N.C., on the right...ours is on the left. #6 shows our finished product, an oil lamp, filled with deer tallow (cooked with prickly pear cactus for to keep it firmer) and utilizing a sage bark wick. Photo #7 shows what can happen if you're not careful.

ANIMAL PARTS

The animal kingdom sure do provide us with an abundance of spare parts...many of which we can use as containers. We will here delve into several of them, beginning with the outside.

Rawhide. Such a variety of containers can be made from the raw hide of the animal that it staggers the imagination.

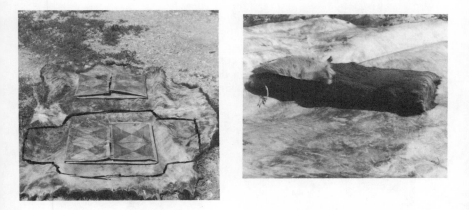

(L) Buffalo rawhide laid out w/a pair of parfletche---traditionally two to a hide. The parfletche was the Plains Indians' suitcase. ALL types of containers can be made from a heavy hide--round/square/rectangular/what have you. They can be held together in any number of ways-sewing/tying/gluing. But, rawhide becomes a oozing mass when wetted and care has to be taken to waterproof anything made from it, or to protect it from moisture. We size (varnish) our products with the juice of the prickly pear. Several other options are available which we won't cover in this book. (R) A container made from the raw skin of a deer, leaving the hair on, for holding our firemaking kit.

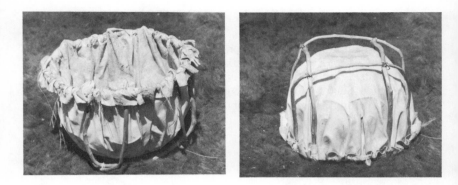

The above two photos show a container which can be used for several purposes. It's simply rawhide of a deer laced to a wooden frame. Most obviously, this could be used for water or hot rock cooking (book #5)

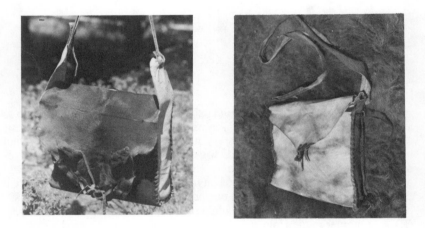

(L) An unborn calf, rawhide, with gussets of rawhide deer, laced together with brain tan. (R) Deer rawhide---gussets and lacing of brain tan.

(L) Deer rawhide container which we use to carry many things, from arrowheads to granola...sewn w/sinew (book #1) and tied w/brain tan. (R) Knife sheath made from buffalo rawhide, laced w/brain tan.

(L) Left, a cow's bladder, after cleaning the "p" out of it, makes a dandy canteen...carrier made of brain tan. The water bucket next to it we have used for several years. Made of a deer skin, we make certain to dry it every night so that it don't begin to rot. The evaporation of the water through the skin keeps it surprisingly cool.

(R) Two heart sacs from cows...to prepare, also w/bladders, let dry--then moisten and manipulate carefully as it dries. Gives good waterproof containers. Sac on left has brain tan sewn on top.

(L) Raw squirrel skin, somewhat made flexible by rubbing while it dried---with wooded cork. (R) Skin inverted, cork inserted, cordage to tie the bottom together and we have a dandy small bag for trap triggers, etc.

A much larger bag can be made from this coyote or most any other animal.

(L) Two turtle shells...many uses for these. Dishes/water carriers/dippers/cups/or in the case of the smaller, deeper one, a fine oil lamp. (R) The leg bone of a bear, filled with a tallow soaked wick and tallow, makes a fine torch.

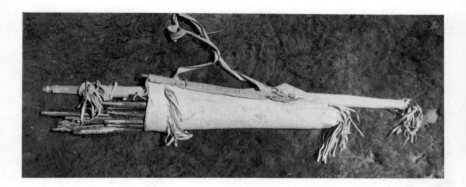

Finished out buckskin makes for many fine containers. Here illustrated is a typical Northern Plains bow case/quiver.

WOOD

Most containers made from wood would (no pun intended here, it just happened) be most associated with bowls for eating, dippers, buckets. In most cases, a container of one piece of wood would (again?) be too heavy and/or prone to breakage. Canoes, dug out logs, would be an exception.

A solid, dry piece of most often a soft wood can be chipped, carved, burned out to make most of the above...one caution though when burning...if moisture remains in the wood, the high temperature of the burning coal can cause the expanding steam to crack the wood (that tip from Steve Watts).

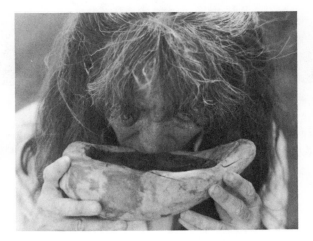

This bowl was made by burning/chipping/scraping.

Now, something a bit different. Many woods, especially it seems soft cottonwood logs, left weathering, rot from the inside out. I don't understand this, but discovered it while gathering punky wood for smoking skins...the insides were well rotted where the outside was still reasonably hard.

Well, note the above photo. Find the "just right" piece, and you can just carefully break away the area that you can use...a container ready to be made.

Now, to the series of pictures. #1 shows about the same tools used in working the stone. #2 shows Geri hard at it...actually the rotted wood separates easily. #3 she smooths out her work. #4 shows where a major crack is in the wood...there were several smaller bug holes. #5 shows fine cordage type material and a small hank of clay---#6 it's mixed together. In #7, she patches the crack, much like caulking a log cabin, sealing the smaller round bug holes as well...tho some of the holes were sealed with only pushing in sticks of the appropriate size.

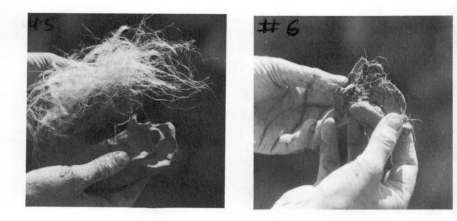

The finished container, holding 1 1/2 to 2 quarts of water---the seals held up real well for several hours and through a hot rock cooking session.

Now you have seen <u>MANY</u> various means to obtain/make containers in the wilds....but more important than that, you have the <u>knowledge of just what to look for</u> when you want to go gathering. For knowing and understanding the principles and characteristics of what you are doing and looking for is more important than knowing only how one or two methods/ materials works...much better than any kit.

8

Primitive Wilderness

Containers

Book 2

PRIMITIVE POTTERY

INTRODUCTION

A reviewer of our books once commented that the only thing missing was a bibliography. Well, the reason for the lack there-of was because mostly of a lack there-of.

When I began writing this series back in the fall/winter of 1985, it was because of the lack of sufficient material that worked. (There was, it turns out, SOME information available---just that it wasn't READILY available.)

This subject, primitive pottery, is an exception. There IS quite a bit of good, solid information out there (that's what I'm told anyhow). But since this has turned into a COMPLETE series of primitive LIVING skills, I find it necessary to include my (our) own work on the subject. A visit to your local library will yield you a lot more information on this subject.

I point out the above only to help explain why there is no bibliography listed here. When a book is in the making in my mind, I try to read nothing on the subject---to keep me from inadvertently plagiarizing some one else.

I do, tho, try to make it a point to recognize anyone who has been of any assistance to us. And here, we have had plenty. We have found that MOST individuals have been more than ready to share with us---and I suppose that right now is a good time to list them.

Margaret (Pegg) Mathewson of California, a real artist in all forms of primitive living.

Steve Watts, Director of Southeastern Native American Studies, Shiele Museum of Natural History, Gastonia, North Carolina

David Wescott, Director of Boulder Outdoor Survival School, Idaho.

Tamera and Larry Bean---he a ranger at Russell Cave National Monument, she a replicator of Southeastern Pottery, Alabama.

Evard H. Gibby, potter from Idaho.

Angelo Garzio, Professor of Art at Kansas State University.

Maria-Louise Sidoroff, Archaeological ceramic replicator, of New Jersey.

The reason that so many people are listed is because we began this project with a limited amount of knowledge---and we really needed help.

Now, with all this in mind, remember that this certainly is not a definitive work on primitive pottery. What this will do is allow one to go out, dig up some dirt (clay) and turn it into a usable container/vessel. Expect some failures. There are a lot of variables here---tho by understanding and following rules, success will follow---for many, on the first try.

You will note that I switch from using I to WE quite frequently. Well I, John, do the actual writing. Geri does about everything else.

Lets get on with it.

February 1990

QUICK RUN THRU

Simply, you need to first find a source of clay.
Dig it,
Wet it if dry.
Clean it,
Form it into a shape, (a bowl in our example here).

Let it dry--- At this stage it can be used under limited and controlled circumstances. It will be very brittle and will dissolve if wetted. Clay, mixed with straw and baked in the sun can and has been used to make bricks (adobe). Bowls can be used for DRY storage. But for most practical applications the item must now be -

Fired---fire will transform the water soluble clay into a material that will allow you to use the bowl not only for the storage of but also the boiling of water.

And it really is about that simple. Lets cover the above steps, maybe adding one or two others as we go.

CLAY

Without getting technical, clay is a type of soil that, (1) when moist becomes plastic, (2) dries hard retaining it's molded shape, and (3) will change characteristics when

Clay, like Geri in this photo, can sometimes be elusive---but it is really rather abundant.

fired, so that it will not dissolve once again when wetted, allowing it's use as a cooking and storage vessel and lots of other utilitarian and fun things.

Most everyone knows what clay is. You just have to find some. It really is a rather abundant earth material. One will most often and easily find clay deposits along stream banks, ponds and road cuts.

If wet when found, a step and time is saved. Just dig back

Before wettin dry clay, it's best to first pound/grind into smaller pieces.

into the vein a bit to get away from surface debris (that will only have to be removed), and dig it up.

If dry, it needs to be rewetted. Lots of ways to do this.

What most "good" potters do is to pound/grind up the clay before adding water (this is to allow for better absorption). Add enough water to completely dissolve the

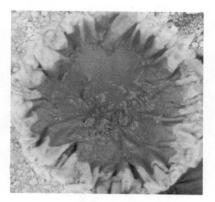

Leftover rubble

The more "approved" method of cleaning. Making into a slurry (L) and pouring off the thinner clay, (R) leaving the stones to sink to the bottom.

particles and to make a "slurry" solution. You want it KINDA thin---the purpose being to allow you to stir the solution well. Let it set for 20 to 30 seconds (allowing the heavier stones, etc. to settle) and then carefully pour off the thinner, silty clay solution into another container. This can

As the mixture is allowed to sit, the clay will settle and the water can then be poured off. The use of the rawhide container speeded this process as moisture was able to evaporate thru the skin.

Further drying is expedited by "pancaking" the clay.

be repeated if necessary. Once about all the impurities seem to be removed, the container is set aside, allowing the heavier clay to settle and occasionally pouring off the lighter water. This can take several days. As the clay begins to thicken, it can be spread out on a smooth surface to speed the drying. When it reaches the right consistency, it's ready to use.

Often when we're in a hurry (I'm always in a hurry it seems) we just mix water and clay, kneading and working it until it's "right", feeling the larger impurities and removing them with our fingers. This works well especially with smaller, quickie bowls when you're rushed. But, it is believed that the longer the clay sits wet, the better.

For working, the moisture content must be "just right". Too wet and it will be too sticky and will slump, not holding it's shape. Too dry and it will crack as you work it. If a little too wet, it can either be spread out to dry some or just worked in your hands, allowing the sun and wind to dry it. This additional working is good for the clay, most notably removing pockets of air. If the clay is just a bit dry, dipping your hands in water, shaking off the excess and working the clay works well.

Clay with just enough moisture to wet. Let set for a short time and then work well with your hands, picking and cleaning

304

NOT ALL CLAYS WILL WORK.

A good, simple test is to roll it pencil thin and tie it into a knot. If it don't break or crack, it's a good candidate. Plasticity is the word.

The amount of shrinkage during drying is also an important factor. Too much can hurt. The addition of temper can sometimes help here.

One clay that we worked with a lot was touted by all who touched and worked with it as having a "great feel". Well, we have never yet gotten a good firing out of it. This was a clay that had all of the outward characteristics of a good usable clay---pliability/shrinkage/feel. But it just wouldn't hold up to the firing---blew apart.

So if you follow all instructions and still have firing problems, change clays.

An easy test to check for pliability

TEMPER

According to Webster's:

Temper: to mix (clay) with water or a modifier (as grog)--

Grog: refractory materials (as crushed pottery and firebricks) used in the manufacture of refractory products (as crucibles) to reduce shrinkage in drying and firing.

First we clean the clay of rubble. Then add more?

We had a lot of questioning to do on this one---and found no one answer. Several points were agreed on by most consultants---but not one would give us a firm definition. Many admitted that they had no idea just exactly what was happening here. Several had theories.

I'll list here what we have noted from others and what we have also come up with.

The temper (grog) is a stable.

The clay is not.

A lot of rubble (stones, etc.) in the fresh dug clay is not, so it needs to be removed.

During drying, and especially firing, the clay will shrink and expand to a certain degree---and here, a little goes a long way---too much and the pot cracks and/or breaks. The tempers helps to keep the vessel (clay) more stable during these periods.

Some clays don't require temper. Others might need up to a one third addition---each clay has it's own special properties.

Small pots require none, or less temper, than larger ones. Large pots have a tendency to slump when building---the addition of temper helps to counteract this.

The intended use of the finished product has some bearing: vessels which will be in and out of the fire (each time experiencing expansion and contraction) will require more than than those used primarily for storage.

The addition of temper actually weakens the pot. More and coarser temper should be added to cooking vessels as it takes the heat shock better.

Geri thinks of temper being the main ingredient and clay just holding it together---kinda like working cement?

And from Steve Watts. On a microscopic level, pottery starts to break down as soon as you start to use it. Miniscule cracks develop every time that the pot is heated or cooled.

Sand

Pot shards as temper

He strongly feels that the temper acts as a stopping point for these cracks---kinda like drilling a hole in a windshield at the end of a crack to stop its' progress.

Now we have some idea of just what temper is and the purpose there-of---what do we use?

SAND/GRIT is usually readily available. But beware of what makes up the sand in your area. Where we live there must be some limestone in it---and our limestone ain't stable. Everytime that we've used it, the pots have blown in firing---limestone in the Southeastern US is different and works.

GRASS, DRIED COW DUNG, and other organic materials.

BROKEN, FIRED POTTERY (SHARDS), crushed fine.

SHELL. Most (all?) shell will work. We have used fresh water mussel successfully. One caution tho---fire, or burn, the shell first. Unfired shell ain't stable---the initial expansion in firing is more than clay---firing stabilizes it.

This list should cover most circumstances---so now lets put it together and make something.

(L) Mussel Shells, being fired.
(R) The fired shell crumbles and is now stable.

308

CONSTRUCTION

Mix the temper and clay to desired proportions---and keep on working it. It can't be worked too much. Slam it. Beat it. Work it in your hands or on a hard surface. Compress everything well---and remove any and all air pockets. If a bit wet, work it till it dries just right---if dry, wet it by dipping your fingers in water. Once the "right" wetness is achieved, I find myself constantly re-wetting by dipping fingers to keep it just right.

At some point take a baseball sized hunk of the mixture and work with that. Work it/work it/work it.

After several minutes, take the ball of clay and begin forcing your fist and/or fingers into it to develop a hollow--- the beginning of the pot. Keep the forming pot moving circularly on the fist...beating/tapping/compressing the walls all the time. Work out cracks. Just keep working it---you'll begin to "feel" the clay.

Start "pulling" clay from the bottom up towards the top. Put your fingers against the inside walls of the pot and pat the outside opposite to further compress. (Here some use a smooth stone on the inside and a wooden "paddle" on the outside---usually wrapping the paddle with cordage to help prevent sticking, called, appropriately, paddling.) All air pockets need to be worked out---they can explode in firing.

In not too many minutes you'll find yourself with a smallish bowl on your hands.

At this point I will take SLIGHTLY dampened fingers over the whole pot, inside and out, smoothing and compressing---being careful to not get it too wet.

Now, if you have the pot the size that you want it (cereal bowl sized?), set it on a piece of bark,or whatever, (easier to move around) and keep it the shade to dry SLOWLY. Fast drying will have the tendency to crack the product. It will now take from a coupla days to a coupla weeks, depending on conditions, of slow drying. Keep it protected. ALL moisture needs to escape...it needs to be bone dry. Any moisture left in it will explode in firing.

Temper added to clay

Mix well. Beat...

Chop... slap...

Pound and fist.

Beginning to form

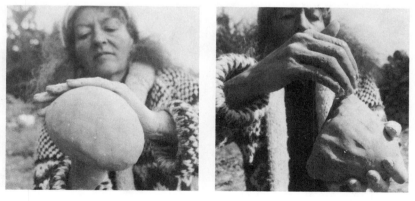

Pat to compress and pull the clay up.

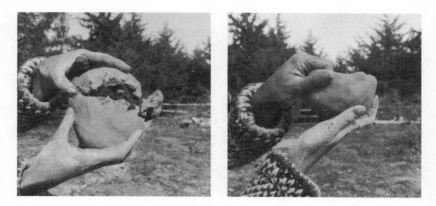

If too much clay, pinch a little off...and continue to form.

Pinching, patting ---

rubbing and smoothing.

Before you know it, you have a bowl.

Set it aside to slowly dry.

Now, if you desire a larger pot, form it this way as large as you can before slumping occurs. When you reach a certain height, the pot will begin to sag, or slump because of its own weight. You now have to let the main body of the pot dry somewhat before adding more weight---but you also need to keep the rim wet so more clay can be "welded" to it.

313

Set the pot in the shade---wet the rim with damp fingers---cover with green leaves or something similar to keep THE RIM from drying too much as the body does. This may take only an hour or so, or maybe even overnight.

When the pot is ready for the addition of more clay, roll out a coil of prepared clay (called "coiling"), the same thickness as the pot walls (less than a quarter inch up to a half inch).

If you wish it larger, roll out a coil and add it on.

This now can be added to the pot. Be careful to not get too much weight at once. You may be able to add more than one coil at a time. Just don't get too rushed. Use your fingernail or a tool of bone/wood/whatever to "draw" the coils together---inside and out. Squeeze and compress it all together to weld into one. In this manner, the pot can be built about as large as you desire.

Pinch, compress and pull it together.

Cover the fresh added clay with wet leaves to keep the rim from drying as the rest of the pot does.

When satisfied, set it aside as you did with the smaller pot. It needs to be DRY---but it needs to dry slowly.As mentioned earlier, this may take up to two weeks.

Well, all rules are not set in clay. Maria-Louise Sidoroff made a large vessel one time---beginning with fresh clay in the morning and fired it that evening. She speeded up the drying process by rotating it around a fire.

After a day or so, under most circumstances, the pots can be handled. We usually turn the pots upside down at some stage in the drying to allow the bottom to dry well.

If you desire to decorate the pot (cordage marks from paddle or rolling a corncob over it, etc.), this should be done prior to drying. When still fresh, or after the initial drying of a day or so (leather dry), lines can be etched into the pot---this CAN be done when dry but seems to work better at the leather dry stage.

Leather dry is also the stage to thin the pot, if desired, by gently scraping away thicker areas, using a piece of bone, stone, or shell.

A very smooth pebble or piece of bone can be used to smooth and burnish the pot --- a good idea for the inside of a pot designed for cooking and/or eating. This can be done at the leather dry or dry stage.

Burnish the inside with a smooth stone for sanitation purposes.

Burnish the outside for decoration.

So what do we have up to now? We've found a source of clay/dug it/cleaned it/dirtied it (added temper)/carefully made a pot/designed it and SLOWLY dried it.

Still one more major step to go---

FIRING

What we have read in the past on primitive pottery concentrated all efforts on building and drying. We were left to assume that if the pot made it thru these stages that we had it made---WRONG!

By just slapping some clay around, you can have success up to this stage---but lose many thru careless firing. Care must be taken!

In PRIMITIVE firing, lots can go wrong---and the pots are very susceptible to breakage at this stage. Some old time primitive potters speak of a failure rate of up to 50%.

Actually, we should refer to the firing in two stages, the pre-firing and the firing.

As the pot heats, it will expand. And any remaining moisture (not ALL leaves in the previous drying) has to be driven out---slowly. So we want to proceed slowly. Gradual heating thru-out. So we pre-heat.

Then the pot must be transferred from indirect heat to direct heat. We lose a lot of them here.

Two other critical stages; (1) when the pot reaches a temperature around boiling (212 F) the remaining UN-NATURAL water leaves and (2) at a temp. of 800 to 900 degrees F, the NATURAL chemical water of the clay is burned out. After this second stage the clay cannot be returned to its original condition and be reworked.

So lets list some firing techniques and tips.

The simplest and most successful method that we've come across I quote here from a paper done by Evard H. Gibby of Idaho:

"The method I like the best and have the most success with is as follows: Scrape a wide shallow depression in the ground, about one inch deep and two feet in diameter. Place a few pebbles on the bottom to lay the over-turned pot on. Lay a piece of cordwood the same diameter as the pot on each side. Leave a space between the logs and the pot. Next lay two same sized pieces in-between the logs and up almost touching the pot. Take a few dried cow chips and crumble

Surrounding with logs (L) and
covering with dried cow manure (R)

covering with more sticks and building into a tipi fire.

Touch it off.

The end result.

them up in small pieces and cover the pot. Then carefully cover the pots with a few more smaller logs. Build a tipi fire on top of the logs and let the whole thing burn down to coals. The pot should be allowed to cool slowly, but cooling can be sped up some by periodically scraping some of the coals away from the pot, and eventually taking the pot out with some sticks."

That's it. One step (no pre-heating). And we can vouch for the fact that it's successful, for small pots at least.

In other firing methods, the pot must first be pre-heated.

Some build a circular fire around pots and gradually move the fire in until finally the pots are actually in the fire itself--- eventually building the fire up with larger pieces of wood and letting it burn for a coupla hours---or instead of using large pieces of wood, constantly replenishing with smaller twigs spaced around/between and above the pots.

Another method is to build a fire and to move the pot(s) closer, turning and rotating them until well pre-heated---then scraping the fire away, laying the pots in the coals/ashes or on an insulated layer of pre-heated rocks or old pottery shards. Let the pots sit a short bit to allow gradual heating up before adding more fire.

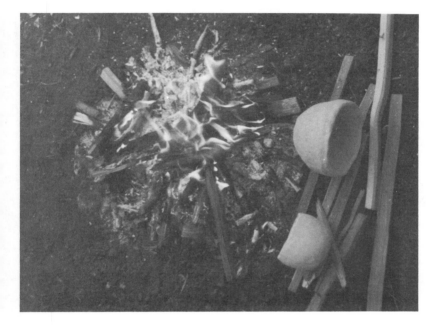

Preheat.

Set on coals a bit and then gradually move the fire in.

Get it closer, higher and hotter ... finally build it over.

From Steve Watts---firing the Catawba way. Pre-heat. Set on coals for a bit---then add pine needles, etc to make for a slow heating. Then begin adding small woods, and then finally larger woods. When burned to coals, re-build. Twice for small pots. Three times for larger ones.

Avoid windy or rain threatening days to fire. A cool draft or drop of rain can ruin your efforts.

One other firing method that we've not found in common use in the states is the use of a PRIMITIVE kiln. This allows one more control in heating gradually. Simply, the kiln is dug into a hillside, a firing chamber below it. The heat and smoke from the fire is tunneled thru the kiln. The ancient Chinese used this extensively, often stairstepping kilns up a hillside, heating from one fire chamber. One must ensure that the firing chamber is of sufficient size to heat the kiln to the required temperature (1200 to 1600 F, color will be from dark red at the lower temp. thru cherry red, bright cherry red to orange at the higher temp.). This temp. should be maintained for two to four hours. The chimney escape should ideally be thru the bottom of the kiln (so as to retain as much heat as possible---which rises, remember?) and then up (see drawing) and the opening needs to be large enough to allow enough draw for the fire to reach the high temperatures required.

I think that this shows you that firing pottery just ain't throwing pots into the fire---but it's not all that difficult either.

Pots are made to use---so use them. The final test is to cook in them. Try to remember the word gradual. Cold water in a hot pot can be disastrous. Same vice/versa. Heat with coals or small flames. When handling hot pots, use leather pot holders or wooden "tongs". Cloth can burst into flames.

Avoid lifting a pot by its rim---you just mite break it off.

And from Maria-Louise Sidoroff, whose expertise in making and using primitive pottery is known internationally: "A well constructed and sound pot will get better with usage", "Using ordinary precautions, the life expectancy would be many, many years".

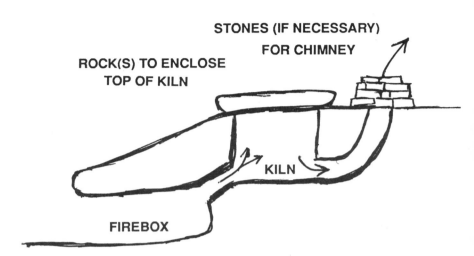

STONES (IF NECESSARY) FOR CHIMNEY

ROCK(S) TO ENCLOSE TOP OF KILN

KILN

FIREBOX

- **Kiln can be lined w/rocks**
- **Pots should be set on rock pillars**
- **Have removable rock at lid for use as peephole to check pots' color (temp).**

The final test ... using it.

ABO POTTERY USE NOTES
Steve Watts
1989

To me the pottery trip is divided into three parts:

1/3 is making it	(Good clay-well prepared, proper temper, and good construction techniques)
1/3 is firing it	(Proper prefiring, and a thorough high firing with adequate cool down time)
1/3 is using it	(proper care and use for storage, cooking, etc.)

After all, using pottery is the main purpose for making it. For a pot to be functional, it must be well made. In other obvious words--the better a pot is constructed and fired, the better it will operate as a cooking vessel.

On a microscopic level, pottery starts to break down as soon as you start to use it. But a well made pot will last thru many cookings if taken care of and treated properly.

Pots should be stored in a secure spot, properly supported and protected from running children, dogs, etc.

An underfired pot (in whole or in part) will fall apart when first used--literally dissolve. Many pots made for display only fall into this underfired category.

Of course shock must be avoided--putting cold water into a hot pot or vice versa.

Some folks suggest filling the pot with water prior to use and letting it stand in the pot long enough to thoroughly saturate the walls before using. Others have suggested preheating and oiling the pot to season it-ala cast iron.

Both of the procedures are probably useful, but my experience is that with a well made pot one simply adds "room temperature" water plus the food to be cooked to the unheated pot and sits it on the fire. Stoke up the flames and cook away.

9

Primitive

Making and using them

INTRODUCTION

Up to now in this series of books we have covered the majority of projects and/or skills necessary for one to live pretty well in comfort in a primitive wilderness situation. But, for the most part we have been using modern tools to do this. What's the purpose of learning a complete series of *primitive* wilderness living skills if one has to resort to modern technology to accomplish them?

Several have asked prior to this about the *primitive* tools necessary ... just why were they saved until last? Well, I guess that it's just our way of teaching. We instruct students here at home in the skills. The skills alone are at times difficult enough to master. We feel, learn the skills, then learn how to do them the hard way.

Hard way? ... well as you'll see in this presentation, hard is the wrong description. Different is the word. Different and more time consuming. But in adapting primitive to our life-styles aren't we trying to get away a little from the time consuming tasks of ordinary life?

Learning to make and use primitive tools in a day to day situation really isn't hard ... but we feel that if one is trying to learn to master not only making tools but also changing your accepted approach to using these tools, then a lot of extra time is required and frustrations are encountered. So we teach the skills first, and then how to accomplish them with primitive tools. As you will see, eventually it all just naturally ties together.

Here, in the order that they touched us, are listed the more prominent figures who have influenced us in our tool making ... primarily flintknapping;

Ernie Peck, who first showed me, John, what to do with a nail and a flake in 1974.

George Stewart, who picked Geri and I out of a crowd and sat us down, showing us the wonders of percussion in 1987.

Brian James, who was the first to begin to try to explain some of these mysteries to us.

Steve Watts ... a very special person in our lives who shows us something new in primitive skills every time that we encounter him.

The list is not by any means limited to only the above. We have been influenced by many in our never ending search ... these are just the ones who have effected us the most *at various stages of our development.* But, what you need really be aware of, is the fact that *we ourselves* made the biggest difference. It was the hundreds, actually *thousands* of hours of *applied practice* that has gotten us to this stage. We say this here only to remind you that you can read everything that you want on any of these subjects, watch all the demonstrations that there are available ... but if you don't just jump right in there and apply yourself, nothing is gonna happen.

A special thanx to our friend *Jeffrey Schmidt* who first proofed this and reminded me (John) just what I had been pounding into his head while teaching him the basics.

November 1991

Tools

... just what do we mean by tools? ... our *hands* are tools. I suppose that for our definition here we will be making tools for our hands to use to do the projects that we have covered so far in this series ... and that will pretty much encompass any project that one is likely to happen upon in a primitive situation.

    1 - They need to be made from materials that one will find in nature ... STONE/SHELL/BONE/ANTLER/HORN/WOOD.

    2 - And just what do we need these tools to do? GOUGE OR POKE/CHOP/POUND/BASH/SPLIT and most importantly ... CUT. Put yourself in a primitive situation without a cutting implement of some sort and you'll not do very well.

    3- Methods of manufacture; FLINTKNAP/PECK/GRIND/BURN.

    So let me break this down now into some semblance of order (order? ... ha!).

    First and most importantly, one needs a cutting tool of some sort ... a pocket knife so to speak. Note all projects that one does in his/her daily regime in the wilds and what tool is the most important? The knife. So we'll begin with what many have been waiting for ...

BASIC FLINTKNAPPING

    Now don't look at some of the photo's here of fine blades and put the book down thinking that "I can never do this". Well, you may be right, maybe you can't. But the tool that you are going to need to cut and chop your way into or out of the woods is within your grasp. Read on.

    There has been a lot taught and some little written about flintknapping (the art of systematically turning stone, flint, into functional tools). *Some* of what we have seen in print is good ... some little *very* good ... but most is just trash. Almost nothing

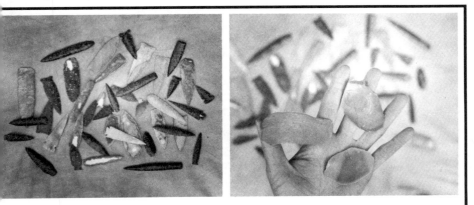

Fancy blades, yes. But in our actual primitive workings they account for probably less than 5% of the actual workload. The easily made flakes (right) do the majority.

generally available to the student of primitive wilderness skills, attends to the ver basics ... the most important aspect of knapping ... the obtaining of the spall or flak to be used *as is* for the tool or to be *turned into* a tool. This first basic function c spalling, making the flake ... is the most important part of knapping. Without it on can travel no further. With it one needs to know no more.

Most certainly we have had help from others learning what knapping w know ... but we have found that even the most willing of teachers wasn't answerin the questions that we didn't even know we needed the answer to. All who kna certainly have some grasp of what the principles are but they either 1) weren conscious of what they were doing (it just came naturally ... it worked), 2) they didn know how to present what they were doing or 3) *they had advanced so far that the had forgotten the importance of the basics.*

A good many of modern flintknappers have learned their skills backward ... the last step first. I, John, know that I did. Here we start at the beginning.

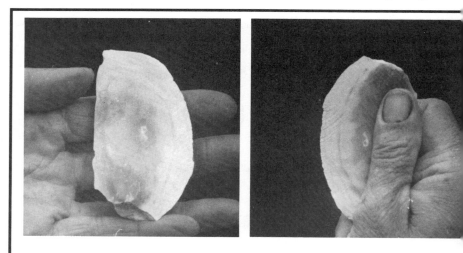

*The functional, simple, easy to
learn, easy to make, one blow tool.*

SAFETY

1) Wear eye protection when working stone. It don't take but one misdirected sharp edge to eliminate sight. 2) Don't breath the dust. Every time that you remove a flake from the stone you will create dust. Once in the lungs, it cuts and creates scar tissue that is there from now on til forever ... and that's a mighty long time. It don't go away like when you quit smoking. Those tiny razor blades do some serious cutting And the resulting scar tissue will eventually kill you if you breath enough of the dus

er a long enough period of time (silicosis). And be aware that the dust not only is
the air, but it also gets into your clothing and whatever. Best don't do it in the house
outside ... let the wind clear the air for you. Most dust masks won't work ... some
ll. Something is better than nothing. 3) You're gonna cut yourself. Keep a supply
bandages handy. If you wish, wear gloves or hold the stone you're working with
iece of leather. We don't anymore but we also occasionally still cut ourselves. Also,
cautious of where the falling flake is gonna land. I've more than once driven a flake
o my leg. Be cautious and you'll be alright. 4) Don't flintknap (especially the
vanced blades) in the company of those with sensitive ears. The accompanying
guage is similar to that of auto mechanics (Geri learned the words from me long
fore she became an active knapper).

FLINT

Just what is flint? Well, according to Webster, flint is a form of quartzite ...
d the description of quartzite is a bit more complicated ... so lets simplify. We'll
np all the stone that we will work "flint like" into one category and call it flint. As
as I know, there are only two sources of true flint in the United States ... the rest
cherts, jaspers, chalcedonies, agates and just plain quartz. To my way of thinking
re goes my theorizing again) most all of these are just various stages of develop-
nt or quality of quartzite (as coal is to diamonds). And quartzite cobbles are pretty
mmon, most as close as your local streambed or roadcut. Generally the better
ality flints are smooth and have a sheen. The poorer ones are more grainy (as in
dy). Most have an outer coating, sorta like a limestone covering, called the cortex

*(Left to Right) 1- Cobble of Dover chert from Tennessee, light brown inside, dark
brown cortex. 2- Cobble of chert from flint hills of Kansas. White limestone cortex,
dark blue banded ring of high quality chert with lighter colored interior of lesser
quality. 3- lens of knife river flint (chalcedony) from North Dakota, rootbeer
colored and translucent. White, hard, smooth cortex.*

331

(cortex is the commonly used term ... corticose is the more proper). Cortexes' va
in workability ... some can be left on and used with the tool ... others are too crumb
and will not do the job at hand. This cortex can hide the flint underneath so you w
need to do some experimenting to find out just what is what (applying the rules th
follow).

Many of you are familiar with obsidian being used in the making
"arrowheads" and other tools. Obsidian is also workable under the same rules th
follow ... it is simply natural glass made by volcanic action. Obsidian is the easie
of these materials to work, it gives the sharpest edge known to man and is great f
beginners and advanced knappers. It's drawbacks? ... it's very brittle and *ver*
dangerous (thousands of tiny dust razor blades to be breathed into your lungs or stuc
into your various body parts). Many flintknappers who have not worked obsidia
kinda knock those who do work with it because of its ease of workability ... *but mo*
of those knocking it would not be able to turn out a fine, thin, long blade from obsidic
without breaking it first. Here we'll call it all flint and just ignore the obsidian ... th
the principles are the same.

One quality that all these rocks have is that they are homogeneous (of th
same composition throughout). Simply put, they are all one ... there is no grain (z
in grain in wood) ... energy will travel equally in *any* direction that it is directed

TECHNIQUES OF WORKING FLINT

There are three generally accepted ways in which one can predictabl
remove flakes from a stone. 1) *Direct percussion,* where you hit the parent roc
directly with either another rock, antler or wood billet. 2) *Indirect percussion* whe
you place a blunt pointed tool (antler tine) at the point of removal of flake from pare
rock and strike this with a billet and 3) *pressure flaking* when you place the antler (
wood) tool against the parent piece and remove a flake by applying pressure. All thre
methods have similar, but different, rules. Here we'll work primarily with the basi
direct percussion, just touching on pressure flaking as a means of re-sharpenin
Pressure flaking can also be very useful in platform preparation.

With direct percussion what we are doing here is striking one rock wit
another (wood/antler/bone are some other tools that can be used). Now, for what w
are doing, about any rock will suffice as a hammerstone ... even the same as the cor
... but this isn't recommended. The better case is to use a sand type stone, but not som
crumbly old piece. It should grip the platform for just a micro-second to allow th
energy to be released smoothly and yet be strong enough to take the abuse ... th
hammerstone deforms as the core bites into it. The harder the flint the harder shoul
be the hammerstone. To remove large flakes from a large nodule one needs a larg
hammerstone. I prefer to work with a fist sized *and smaller* hammerstone for m
general work as this fits comfortably in my hand and seems easier *for me.* The smalle
the hammerstone the more force necessary for flake removal and the more forc

xerted, the less the accuracy. And accuracy is important. You will discover that if the
)ck is properly struck, the flake will separate easily.

RULES

In order for one to make finely flaked, long, thin blades, you first must learn
many, many rules and have (usually) years of experience. In order for you to make
he stone tool necessary to perform the functions outlined earlier you need be aware
f only two rules ... and you can be turning out tools (flakes) almost immediately. This
as been argued by one of the countries foremost knappers but I have proved him
rong many times. In fact after one 45 minute (plus or minus) session, there were
ree students out of the 15 present doing just that ... and they were on average eleven
ears of age! The rest didn't seem to care.

Two rules. Pay attention. Your practice will be your finished tool. Two rules
(repeat myself purposely), one more important than the other. 1) The *cone*, and 2)
he *platform*, *the cone being the more important.*

1) The **cone** - determines how rock will break when struck. Flint
reaks conchoidally ... the instant that a force strikes the surface of the flint, the energy
s transmitted into a <u>cone</u> radiating at about 120°. The break in the stone pretty much
ollows this cone. The significance of the cone is that it determines at what angle and
where you must strike a blow in order to remove a particular chunk of stone.

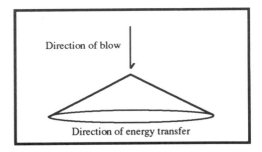

2) The **platform** - *is the surface that the blow is delivered to.* It must
ave a particular shape or the blow will be ineffective. The platform cannot be
rumbly or fragile ... if so the stone will crumble when struck rather than fracture
leanly. The platform is the edge of the stone forming an angle of ***less than 90°***. The
mportance of the platform is that it determines whether or not a blow will produce
flake at all. You can beat all day on an obtuse angle (more than 90°) and not produce
predictable flake ... or strike a weak platform and ruin it. We will note various
latforms in the following text and photos.

You can know only the concept of the cone and produce tools - you can know
nly the platform and not. Know and be proficient with both and you are what I

consider a flintknapper. You will be able to remove flakes from a stone in a predictable manner ... conversely, you will be able to predict what is left behind. You will be in control.

Each time you remove a flake you need to prepare a new platform for the removal of another flake from the same area. At each stage, before a blow is struck, you need to study the rock and ask yourself what must be the angle of the blow to the core to remove a targeted flake ... and insure yourself of a good, solid striking surface (platform).

The cone ... the all important cone. All knappers are well aware of it ... it's a physical law ... you can't flintknap without some knowledge of it. There are literally hundreds of rules that one must follow in the course of advanced flintknapping ... but you will find that a good share of them are dictated because of the cone.

Remember, the line of force is not a straight cleavage, <u>it is a circular cone</u> (note photo's). This line of force, as it were, I can't stress to you enough. Once you become aware of what it is that I'm saying, a little light will go "Bingo" and you'll find yourself with a damn good comprehension of what is happening. Like most other primitive skills, there ain't no magical formula ... just regular laws of physics that once understood (along with lots of practice) will enable you to be in charge.

When striking a blade from a core, the natural tendency is to want to strike in line with the intended blade to be removed (dotted line) ... but ... due to the conchoidal fracture principle the energy will then go too deeply into the stone - you want it to more or less "skim the surface". Left above photo shows the lines of force - the right above one shows the results.

90°

120°

Ang
of
blo

o

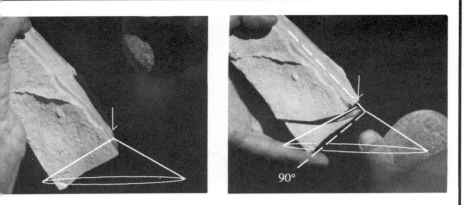

Note the angle that the core is held in relation to the blow. Most beginners have the tendency to not compensate enough ... *it's a pretty severe angle*. Also note in the right photo how the flake tends to naturally curve outward from the **cone** and into the **core**. NOTE THE SURFACE THAT IS STRUCK BY THE HAMMERSTONE - THE PLATFORM - IT IS SOLID WITH NO WEAK OVERHANGS.

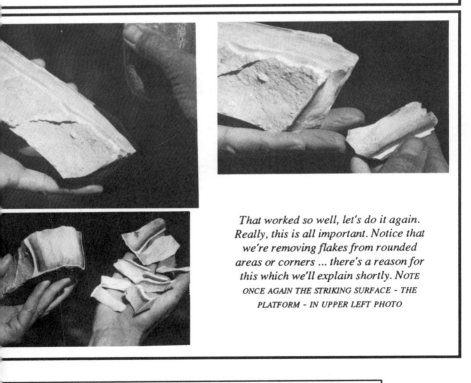

That worked so well, let's do it again. Really, this is all important. Notice that we're removing flakes from rounded areas or corners ... there's a reason for this which we'll explain shortly. NOTE ONCE AGAIN THE STRIKING SURFACE - THE PLATFORM - IN UPPER LEFT PHOTO

Note (Left) that when the angle reaches or becomes greater than 90°, the energy runs too deeply into the stone for flake removal.

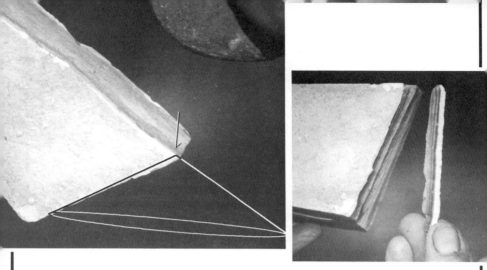

In this set of photos we'll illustrate the removal of thin and thick blades - thin for surgical slicing and thick for scraping or chopping. Note that the angle and placement of blow are the determining factors. Angle here shows clearly. Blow placement - closer to the edge for thin (above) ... further in for thicker (below).

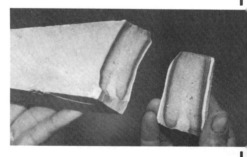

Oops! ... too severe an angle..

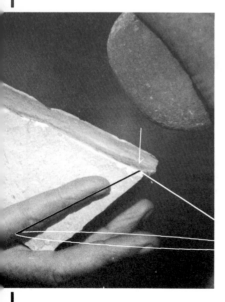

Try again with better results on the other corner.

*(Top left) A **wide**, long, thin blade is removed by striking nearer the edge but further "around the corner" into the straight plane and holding the core at a more extreme angle giving us a sharp blade (upper right) but also one which will dull easily.*

(Left) The edge is resharpened by pressure flaking, here using a rounded piece of hard, dead wood, in this case, dogwood. Pressure flaking is where most folks begin their learning of flintknapping ... where it actually is the final phase. It is, as the name implies, applying pressure to the piece until a flake pops off the opposite side. Here, in a primitive situation, wood is used. Antler or bone make for better tools. To protect the hand, a leather pad is used. (Below) The resulting sharpened edge.

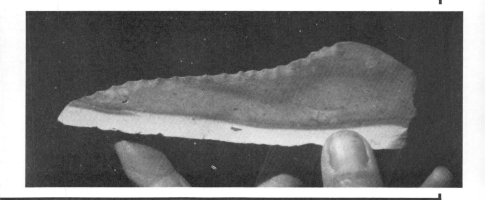

Removing flakes to leave tool behind ...

A natural lens of chert (left) ... the cortex in this instance is crumbly and so its edge is neither sharp nor durable ... so we remove a series of flakes (left) to give us a better edge (below). You will note that this particular tool is used much throughout this book on various projects.

The two photo's above accentuate well the cone shaped flake. This is accomplished by striking a bit further back on the PLATFORM *and allowing the energy to flow deeper into the stone by not angling it quite so much ... this gives a more solid edged tool for scraping, and chopping.*

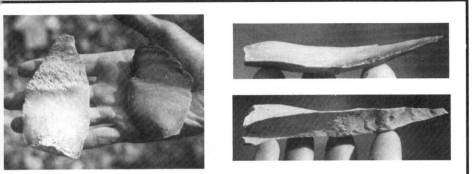

Good examples of average working flake tools. (Upper left) shows "inside" of the flakes ... the sides removed from next to the core. The lower is the end that was struck. (Upper right) Illustrates side views of the same flakes - the left side being the side "struck" (platform). Note that no lines are straight. The line of force, as it travels, tends to bend outward, away from the line of initial force (cone) and into the parent rock (core).

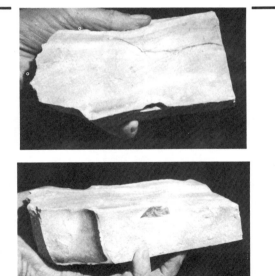

Three photo's (above) illustrate well why a corner or rounded face is necessary for predictable flake removal. The mass of the core simply holds onto the flake ... the sides won't release it ...
...tho ...
(Right) You sometimes can call a usable blade from a straight edge.

PLATFORMS

(Upper right) Unprepared platform from top and side view. Thin, weak overhang will collapse before dissipating energy properly. To clean up this weak overhang, pull your hammerstone as shown (above), (big time knappers use an abrasive grinding wheel found at the local hardware store for this - use what you have available ... oftentimes only your hammerstone) - remembering that the conchoidal principle is still at work here. (Above right) Resulting prepared platform.

Another view of platform preparation. Top unprepared, bottom ready to go.

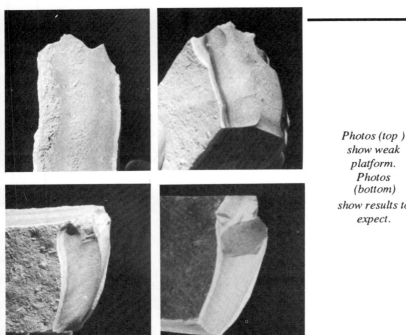

Photos (top) show weak platform. Photos (bottom) show results to expect.

SUPPORT

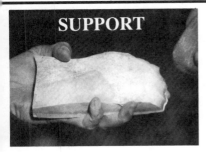

We have established that when you strike a rock the energy is transmitted conchoidally - into a cone. But, there are some variances. If you were to strike a blade from an end of a long, slender piece, shock waves from the blow go traveling thru the rock haphazardly. If the rock were not supported properly, these haphazard (or maybe not so haphazard) shock waves just may snap the piece in two at the unsupported end. So, one does need to be aware of this for some of our basic work. Note photos.

Three common ways to support a piece. 1 (Above) Here the hand is doing the supporting, tho this particular piece is almost too long for free hand support. The far end is held against the palm while the fingers hold the worked end.

2 (Right) Lay the piece on your thigh ... in this case without a pad, as would be the case in the field. Most knappers use a thick leather pad. In this photo the worked end alone is resting on the thigh while the other end is simply "supported" by the knappers other hand. The entire piece could be resting on the thigh.

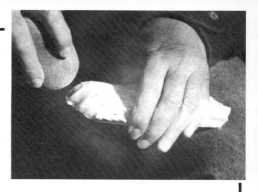

3) In this case, the worked end is free while the other end is supported by being pushed tightly into the thigh.

DISCOIDAL

When working with oval, flattish quartzite cobbles it sometimes is easiest to "get into" the rock or to simply remove a blade using a method taught by Boulder Outdoor Survival School and coined "discoidal". In this operation a cobble (about six inches long, 4 inches wide and 2 inches deep ideally sized) is swung onto an anvil stone (something substantially larger and harder) striking near the end of the cobble.

This will remove a roundish sharp flake. This is the same concept that we have already discussed, only in reverse ... all angles the same. By using the space left from the flake removed as a platform, another flake can then be removed from the reverse side by conventional percussion ... and then another ... giving you a handy hand ax, one of mankinds oldest stone tools.

With discoidal, the flake is removed by the same rules ... only the hammerstone here is the anvil. Two tools ... the flake and the core. Utilizing the platform formed with the flake removal, a hand ax is readily created by simply removing more flakes (knives).

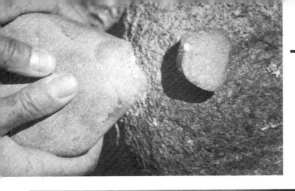

*A flake knife tool
(left) and a handaxe
(below).*

BI-POLAR

When smaller cobbles similar to those just described above are the only stone available, you are still not without a knife. By taking the flattest of these and placing it up-ended on an anvil rock, you can split these neatly in two by striking a blow on the top. What this does is drive the energy directly through the stone to the anvil and then back up. Some stones are definitely harder than others and several blows may be indicated ... watch those fingers. It's easy to smash them.

With normal percussion flake removal, an angle of less than 90° is necessary (as noted before). What then to do if all you have is egg shaped rocks? One answer is to simply throw one against another and hope for the best. But to do it like the "big boys", and retain some control, we can turn to bi-polar here also. My limited

343

experience with this using larger pieces (mostly obsidian) has shown that the drawings of an egg shaped rock being hit bi-polar on an anvil rock don't neatly split in two in reality. Direct your blow carefully and be certain to close your eyes just prior to contact (even with eye protection). Pieces of sharp stone can and will be flying all over the place ... but you *will* have basically two halves, giving you the beginning of a core for flake removal.

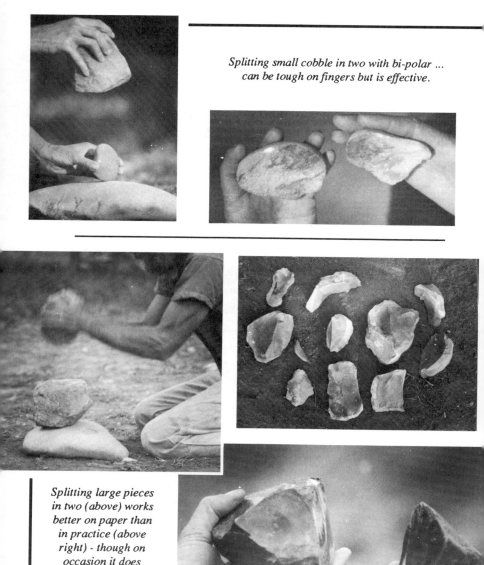

*Splitting small cobble in two with bi-polar ...
can be tough on fingers but is effective.*

*Splitting large pieces
in two (above) works
better on paper than
in practice (above
right) - though on
occasion it does
succeed (right).*

Some notes;

It is difficult to remove long flakes from a flat surface (because the energy is cone shaped and tends also to curve outwards).

Flakes will tend to follow ridge lines (certainly as there is no mass on either side to prohibit the cone from releasing).

It is difficult to impossible to shoot flakes thru a valley. The energy will stop at the far side of the first ridge and most probably hinge (abrupt line of stoppage). It is just about as hard to run a flake through a "hill" (over 90°).

Good practice is to draw the projected flake to be removed on the stone with chalk ... and then carefully study the results. This will eliminate haphazard banging (*tip from Scott Silsby*).

The ideal flake can be removed from a surface which is off a platform of less than 90° (at and above 90° the energy is shot too deeply into the "mass" of the stone), the outer surface runs smoothly with no abrupt "hills" or "valleys" to impede the energy flow, and the surface being somewhat rounded (as with a ball).

RECOMMENDED

... once you have the understanding of the concepts placed forth here, some of you will want to advance even further. The only complete book that I'm aware of that is worth its salt is **"The Art of Flintknapping"** by D.C. Waldorf. The only drawback that I know of with this book is the fact that it doesn't begin basic enough (a good reason for this book). The first time or two that I went through it I was ready to trash it ... I simply wasn't able to comprehend what it was that he was saying ... too advanced. But, once I got some basic understandings under my belt, I understood more and more. I still read it occasionally and each time pick up more. *Get it.* Another "primer" on this subject is "Flintknapping - the art of making stone tools" - by Paul Hellweg. Some sources that handle these are;

Crazy Crow Trading Post
POB 314
Denison, Texas 75020

James D. Hayden
Purveyor of fine books
88360 Charly Lane
Springfield, Oregon 97477

Three Rivers Archery
130 S. Clinton St.
Fort Wayne, IN 46802

Ne Shutsa Traders
Box 186
Haven, Kansas 67543

Three Rivers Archery
130 S. Clinton
Fort Wayne, Indiana 46802

Track of the Wolf
Box "Y"
Osseo, Minnesota 55369

Whew ... !

I'm sure glad that that's over with. Not that the subject is so difficult, as you have seen, but just finding the right words and putting them with the right photo's to make it all gel. So, lets proceed.

Trying to figure some sort of sequence for what follows has been about as time consuming as doing it. You'll find that much of what we are putting forward from here out ties back to our basic stone working (knapping) ... also that working with one resource requires on occasion working with another. It's that damn old *circle* of primitive technology.

What we have done now is just kinda laid out the photo's of what we have done for this book ... and I'll write around them as they speak much better than any words or drawings. Since we have been concentrating on sharp edges, lets continue with ...

SHELL

Shell, thick ones or thin ones, can be utilized in many ways as tools. Heavier ones can actually take quite a bit of abuse as choppers or scrapers but probably the most common use would be as a cutter of some sorts.

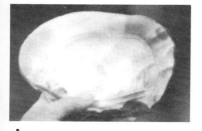
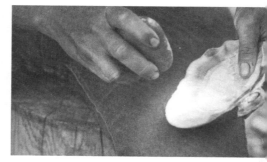

Heavier shell is here percussed with a hammerstone into a sharp, serrated edge.

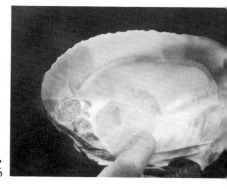

346

*Shell here is thinner ... (Upper left) being pressure flaked to a
serrated edge (upper right and right). Below is raw shell
(left) and other half (right) that has simply been ground to an
edge on sandstone.*

SANDSTONE

*Various grits and hardnesses of sandstone are very important tools ...
in the production of tools.*

HEAVY BLUNT INSTRUMENTS

Lots of uses for a tool such as this ... from driving stakes to mashing nuts. Of course, the easiest is to simply grab the nearest rock or piece of wood and bash away. Here we'll refine those just a bit.

═══ WOOD ═══

Chopping (left) with handaxe of tough quartzite, this hard piece of osage orange took less than 10 minutes to score deep enough to ... break (right) where we wanted it to. Finished club (center) has had the hand grip chopped to a size more suitable to our hands.

═══ STONE ═══

Rocks can, of course, be used as is. But one can also shape them to about any shape that one desires by pecking ... continual hitting with a harder rock. Not difficult, but time consuming. We illustrate here the pecking of a groove into a very hard piece of rock utilizing an even harder piece of jasper. Holding the piece in your hand or on your leg is recommended as the pecked rock may just break in two if it is placed onto a hard surface. Hafting will be illustrated further along.

BONE AND ANTLER

Antler, and especially bone, are common finds of any gatherer. All animals die and unlike humans, their remains are allowed to renourish the Earth from whence they came. If one can come upon them before they disintegrate, these can be dandy additions to any tool kit.

Knives, projectile points, wedges, scrapers, needles, fishhooks, and awls are just a few of the many uses of these items.

The most common and easiest way to downsize bone and antler into workable sizes for most tools is simply to bash them with a blunt instrument ... tho this is certainly not the most reliable method. If time and patience permit, scoring (cutting a line into the bone along which you desire the break to occur) beforehand can bend the odds in your favor as to which direction the break may happen ... the deeper the score the better. Some real fine, long awls and needles have come from leg bones that had been properly scored lengthways. Moist heat will temporarily soften them making scoring and cutting much easier ... tho, with antler anyhow, overboiling will weaken it considerably. Scraping with a stone blade and rubbing on sandstone will add the finishing touch and, in fact, a piece of sandstone is oftentimes the only tool necessary to finish out a piece.

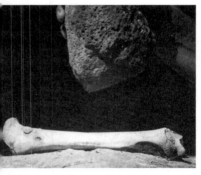 

BONE

Using a rock as our basher (upper left) we reduce this deer leg bone into more manageable pieces (upper right). Some grinding on sandstone (lower left) gives us a nice awl, projectile point or knife and a fishhook (lower right). Simple bashing and grinding gave us these tools in just a matter of minutes.

ANTLER

Antler is very similar to bone in characteristics and workability ... tho thru our own personal experiences we have found that antler is more flexible than bone and so will take a bit more abuse. Also, it seems that the molecular structure of antler is tighter than that of bone so that we can get sharper cutting edges. Horn, which we show no examples of here, seems to be even more flexible and tighter in molecular structure. (We define *antler* as the outer projection growing from the heads of certain animals such as elk and deer ... *horn* as the outer sheathing of antler on such animals as cow, buffalo and sheep.) Shown here are just a couple of examples of things to make from antler.

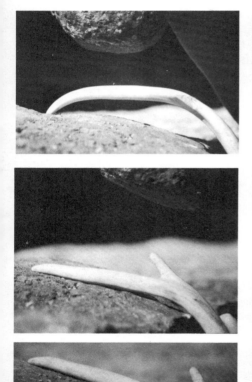

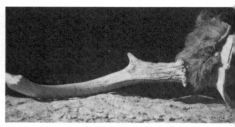

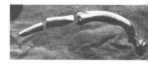

(Right top) Antler from skull cap to where we just broke it ... (middle) same piece after bashing off skull cap and grinding on sandstone to make billet for percussion flaking flint. (Bottom left) shows two small wedges or chisels and (bottom right) how it all places together.

(Left top) Wrong way to break deer antler - tip will break off, we know not where. (Middle) Better way ... note where gap under antler is ... where it does break (bottom).

Elk antler. (Top) about to strike with rock at score mark. (Middle) where it broke ... right at the score. The underside of the antler broke out of the score ... this could've been corrected by scoring deeper. (Bottom) what a few minutes of grinding on sandstone accomplished to turn this into a fine wedge.

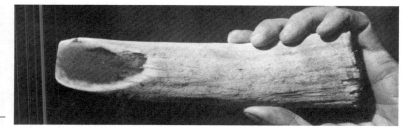

DIGGING STICK

One of mankinds' oldest tools is the digging stick ... simply a pointed stick that was used as for digging or prying. It, of course, requires the use of tools in making.

Which end to use ... ?

... and then chopping ...

... FIRE ...,

... hardens the end by driving out moisture and also makes it easier to point.

... more chopping ...

... grinding on sandstone.

A
very functional,
durable,
hard pointed
digging stick.

A WOODEN AWL

Whilst still working with wood, lets do another kinda quickie project ... again using tools to make another.

Using our trusty quartzite handaxe and wooden maul (left), we split the leftover end of our digging stick, (right) chop it to shape with a flint axe, (below left) shave it further with the sharp flint and finally (below right) grind it on sandstone to end with (bottom) a finished awl or possible needle utilizing the natural knothole.

Celt

In previous pages you have seen the making and using of choppers made from quartzite and flint. Here we will show another common approach to the making of an axe ... the celt. Made from what most refer to as "*greenstone*" (its more common color in certain areas), the stone is actually a mixture of minerals (basalt, jade, and hematite are some common celt meterials... each locale has it's own). It can be found almost anywhere, located often as cobbles but also may be found in veins. The **property** that we are looking for is a certain degree of hardness and smoothness so that the piece will *grind* down to a sharp edge but will also take abuse. We want a hard, dense, tough rock. Several break conchoidally, which in many cases ... such as here ... helps in reduction. One test is to remove a flake, grind and polish it and then attempt to break it with your hands. Some of these stones will not flake and in this case pecking (with another, harder rock) may be in order. A knapped axe is truly functional but a ground celt will hold its edge better and so is worth the extra time spent in production. The celt illustrated here took right at eight hours to make.

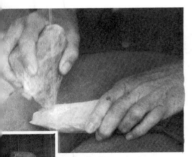

Breaking in two (left) a large lens of "greenstone" by laying it at the edge of a rock and placing a well struck (and lucky) blow using a hammerstone and then reducing by percussion (right) to a more manageable size.

When presented with certain high areas, pecking (left) can be the solution to more quickly removing material. Most time will be spent in grinding and polishing (right) on various surfaces of sandstone.

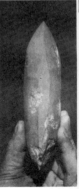

Finished celt has (left) flattish top to help prevent splitting of handle, tapering towards the rear (middle) so as to fit into hole in handle and a proper angle at the cutting edge (right) ... too thin an angle will break too easily and too abrupt will not cut as well.

HAFTING

The placing of an axe, celt or other tool onto a handle can really make your work easier ... and it's not all that difficult to do once you become familiar with working with the various natural materials. Since we just made a celt, lets now haft it.

(Left to right) The roughed out handle after being reduced by fire and chopping - beginning to burn hole by placing a coal and blowing thru tube - directing the burning by blowing onto firebrand. Burning the hole can be tricky. Once the area is charred, it will ignite and burn readily. To prevent burning where you don't want to, remove the char ... the hard wood is harder to ignite. You can also place water or a slurry of clay in areas you don't want to burn. When the hole becomes deep enough, the fire starves for oxygen and one needs to blow constantly. You can burn from the opposite direction after reaching half way.

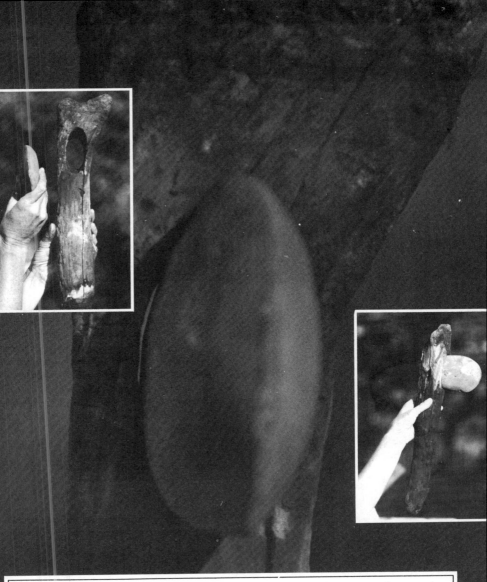

Sizing of the celt to the hole is critical. Contacts at the top and bottom must be spread evenly the entire thickness ... the surfaces flat to help prevent splitting out of the handle. I like to include a "Y" at the top of the handle as I find this stronger ... leave about two inches at the top. Some woods split easier than others and it's wise to check this out before you get four to six hours invested into making the handle (this handle took four plus hours to make). Elm yes ... cedar no. The weight of the wood is kind've important also ... the heavier making for less work when chopping. The hole is tapered as is the celt so that friction from use seats it tight. A gap of at least 1/16th of an inch needs to be left at the sides - otherwise the celt will spread the handle out thereby splitting it. ⁰A special thanx here to **Scott Silsby** for his efforts in helping me try to explain the qualities of "greenstone" ... a not so easy task.

Here we have hafted the "masher" (large photo) that we pecked on page 22 by simply cording heavy rawhide and wrapping it around the groove and braiding the "handle" ... stout enough for driving stakes and mashing foodstuffs. On smaller grooved hammers/axes (inset photos left) we have wrapped the handle itself around the stone ... twice on the left one and once on the right one. Most green saplings or limbs are very flexible and are made even more so by boiling or heating for a short period. They have then been held in place with natural fiber cordage ... the one on right permanently to be used as is and the one on the left to be reinforced with a light rawhide wrapping sewn on with sinew (as in inset photos right).

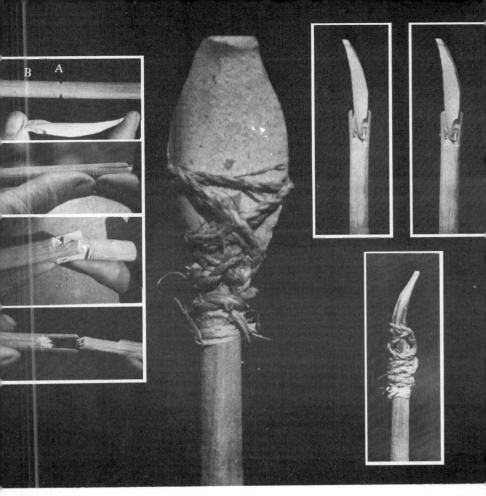

There are several ways to mount a point to a stick. You can (and we have) saw into the end
with a flake - the most time consuming. You also can simply split the piece in two, carve out
a channel for the blade and then bind it all together, gluing it if you have something. The
easiest that we know of, but not always applicable, is this trick discovered by Larry **Dean**
Olsen. Pay special close attention to this group of photo's. (**Left**, top to bottom) - 1) Blade is
laid alongside shaft and notches are cut (A) _leaving behind the size you want the groove to
be_. A thin line is cut (B) where split is to stop (depth of groove). 2) The notch is carefully
split ... both sides ... to line (B). 3) Shaft is turned and the groove is "popped" out by bending
in both directions from line (B). Pay special attention to where the fingers and thumbs are
placed for pressure points. If you're not careful the shaft will simply break at its weakest
point ... the notches. 4) The results.

(**Right**) Once groove is made it's best to custom fit the piece, especially stone. Remember, no
straight lines with stone flakes. (Top left) The initial fit ... by trimming with a sharp blade the
piece is made to fit better (top right). The resulting knife (bottom) lashed into place with
natural fiber cordage may not be the strongest but will still do a number of chores. Setting
the piece with pitch or hide glue would really make it durable.

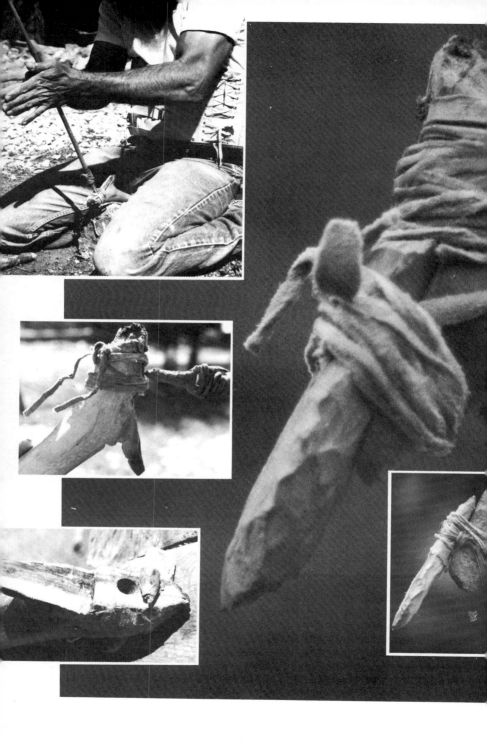

ADZE

The adze is a specialized tool used for trimming and shaping wood.

The blade itself can be made from "greenstone" and ground **or** flaked from flint, as here. It is mounted opposite from an axe, at right angles to the handle. Unlike the axe, the blade will be more flat on one side than the other allowing more careful removal of wood. Shown are two methods of attaching the blade to a handle.

(Left inset, top to bottom) In this case the blade sits on a solid platform of the handle ... and it can break off. Here I am repairing just that by having glued the separated platform back on and lashing it in place ... then drilling a hole with a hand drill mounted with a stone point and plugging the hole with a carved piece of hardwood glued in place. The finished repair job is background photo and it has done a lot of work since.

Another method of attaching the blade (lower center inset) is to wrap it in rawhide or buckskin for cushion and tying that to a flat ended handle. This works well by absorbing a lot of the shock .

Two drills (below inset) with stone tips hafted as shown on page 33, the longer a hand drill and the shorter for use with the bow drill.

VISE

We're kinda stepping up in the world now ... a vise of all things. This trick was shown to us by a flintknapper and old time trapper from Colorado by the name of George Stewart. The one illustrated here is on a small scale and is shown holding an arrow shaft sized stick ... but this could all be up-scaled and used for bows, etc.

Drive a stake into the ground ...   *... split it down about six inches ...*   *... tie securely at bottom of split to keep it from opening too wide.*

Make a loop of strong cordage near the top, insert a stick and twist it tight to hold whatever. Tie or otherwise secure the bottom of the leverage stick.

362

WORKING WITH THE TOOLS

Up to now in this book we have dwelt primarily with the making of tools although many also utilized some previously made ones. Now we are going to do a coupla projects which are aimed only at *using* them.

One project that covers most primitive tool usages is the bow ... so we'll head to the timber in a bit and show you how to do this with tools we have made up to now.

We stress with students the importance of being capable of heading to the wilds and making a fire (book # 2, ***Primitive Fire & Cordage***) with nothing but what is available ... something, of course, not always possible. This is what we will cover first.

Preparing a fire board and hand drill ...

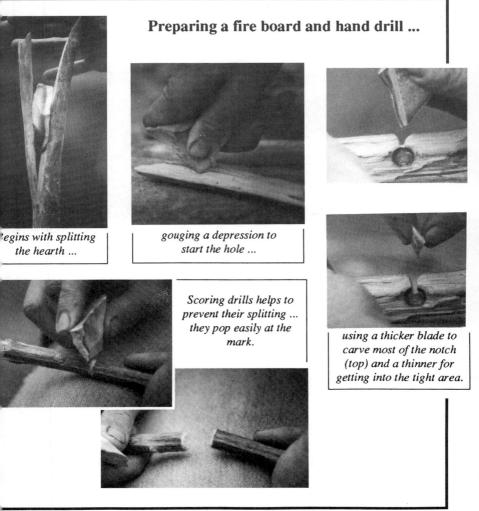

...egins with splitting the hearth ...

gouging a depression to start the hole ...

Scoring drills helps to prevent their splitting ... they pop easily at the mark.

using a thicker blade to carve most of the notch (top) and a thinner for getting into the tight area.

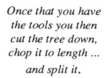
Once that you have the tools you then cut the tree down, chop it to length ... and split it.

... scrape bark off using flake if necessary ...

... cut to length ...

... chop to shape using either handaxe or adze ...

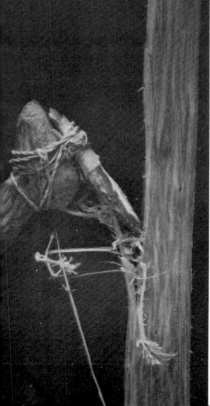

,,, split off any excess ...

*... at some point we need to line
the bow out, here using
charcoal.*

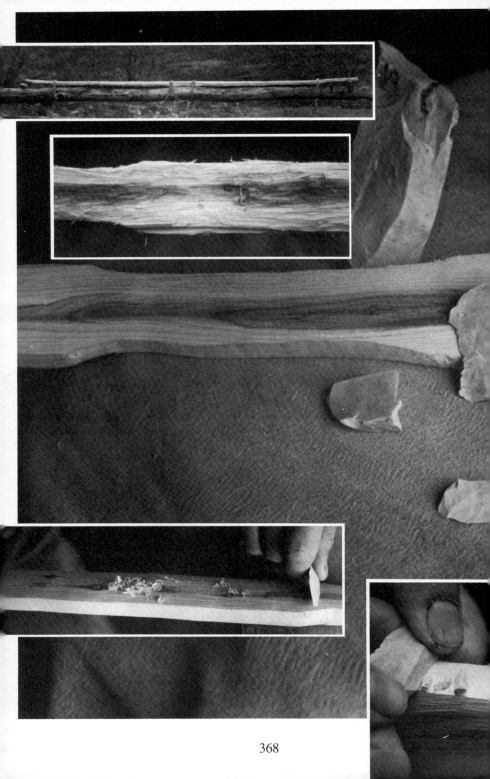

Up to now we've worked with green wood. To cure it out we now tie it (upper left top) in whatever position that we desire the final bow to take ... (this "quickie" bow procedure we learned from our good friend **Jim Riggs** of Oregon) ... and let it dry from several days to more than a week depending on the wood - the denser the wood the longer - in this case we let this piece of eastern red cedar ... actually a juniper ... dry for one week in our hot basement. At this point (upper left bottom) the roughed out bow is just that ... rough. But - (below left) with some little scraping, (below center) some careful cutting - here of the grip - and (below right) sanding with stone, we end up with (full page photo) a pretty much finished out piece - surrounded by just some of the flake tools used.

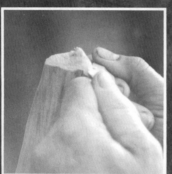

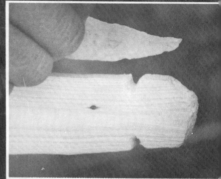

*There are any number of positions for you to experiment working in. (Sequence upper left) - Here Geri buries one end of the bow (upper left) into her belly and the other into a secure area in a rock and draws the flake towards her to remove wood shavings in a hurry ... she then (upper right) makes final cut to length with adze and (lower left) shapes up end with a sharp flake before (lower right) cutting notches. (Background and below) The finished bow. For more detailed instructions on the making of bows refer to our book # 3, **Makin' Meat-1, The Primitive Bow and Arrow** in the **Prairie Wolf** series.*

FINIS

So there you have it. You'll note that in the section on flintknapping that there was little to no mention of "arrowheads" or other projectile points. Well, there is a reason for this which I hope that you have picked up on by now ... *they just aren't that important in primitive living*. A sharpened stick will kill just as certainly as any "arrowhead" **if properly placed** and the making of projectile points is a schooling of its own usually requiring years. The tools that we stress as important require no more time than what it took you to read this book and to take a little sit down to apply.

With the exception of just a few items interspersed, everything was made for the production of this book. The celt and handle required over 12 hours total and the bow took one afternoon to cut and prepare to tying down and an additional better part of a day to finish out. The majority of the rest were made in one afternoon. This ain't to brag ... just to reinforce to you that this really isn't all that difficult. If we can do it, anyone can.

Since we have a page and a half of white space left over, we'll just show you a few other objects that we have made using the techniques shown in this book.

─── WOODEN BOWL ───

This bowl was made from a piece of aspen following guidelines set forth in this book ... stone tools and friction made fires.

Something often forgotten when speaking of tools are food preparation items. Both the Mano/metate and the mortar/pestle are more than just a little useful when living primitively when it comes to grinding of staple items such as seeds, acorns and corn.

MANO AND METATE

This small metate and accompanying mano of pumice (or basalt?) was made by Geri and I for use in our small camps and demonstrations. The depression was created simply by grinding with the mano.

MORTAR AND PESTLE

The above mortar was made in just a few hours by pecking with the same piece of jasper shown on page 22.

374

10
PRIMITIVE
SEMI-PERMANENT

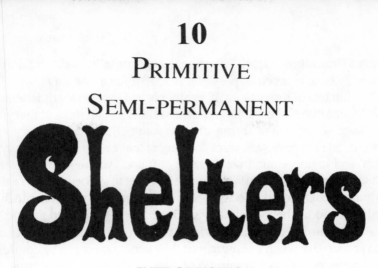

INTRODUCTION

Some of my fondest memories are of sitting in a shelter tucked under pine trees or in a forest of oaks and other hardwoods - the wind howling - freezing rain or snow - a blazing fire and a warm drink.

We have seen and heard much lately on shelters from others with outdoor backgrounds. When one hears that we are working on a book on shelters almost to a person the suggestion arises that we must include the basic ... what many call ... the *debris* shelter.

Let me digress just a bit on the *debris* shelter. For those who don't know of what I speak, this is not much more than a glorified pile of leaves, grass and sticks that one crawls into, much like a sleeping bag. It insulates one from whatever one wants to be insulated from. It does do it well. Everyone, it seems, wants this.

Well, we won't more than just touch on it. Why? ... Well, because when we were kids ... and also with just about any kid who grew up around trees of some sort and who wasn't (*isn't* also as we speak of the kids of today too) afraid of dirt ... it was just natural to build a shelter of this type. Imagination and skill it just don't take.

I think of three instances of where this shelter comes in handy. 1) A true survival situation where one just don't have the time to complete a better shelter, *including making a fire.* 2) In a situation where the instructor doesn't want to take the time and effort to show the student better housing. 3) Where the instructor doesn't know anything more.

If it sounds as if I'm knocking this basic shelter, well, I guess that I kinda am. For survival where nothing else exists it works. Not much more time is needed to instruct one than what is already presented here.

Simply a large pile of "debris" that one crawls into to insulate - retaining one's body heat as much as possible. It actually *is* a sleeping bag.

￢ But lots of restrictions. If weather is bad (reason for the shelter) one is locked into his bed. If he ventures out he'll end up wet and that you don't want when you're trying to stay warm. So in a true survival situation, one is pretty well stuck looking at leaves and grasses at nose length and laying around waiting to get found (you're also insulated from sound and well camoflaged) or the weather to get better. If, like the vast majority of modern woodspeople you have *placed* yourself into this woods situation, when you finally get bored, you get up and go home.

I, John, have been accused most of life of being somewhat crazy ... maybe so. But when I venture into the elements, I try to be comfortable. I have spent the vast majority of my life "camping out" during the winter months ... growing up in the mountainous Southern Tier of New York State and also for the last 20 plus years here in Kansas. Winters get cold. I many times think that people felt that when I ventured out I just kinda curled up in a convenient snowbank. I love winters and cold weather. But I hate being cold and miserable. A good shelter makes for good comfortable *living* out of doors.

If one is without any bedding, the debris shelter is your bedding. But don't make it your house also. Build something to live in while you're up and about and can attend a fire - use the litter for a sleeping bag.

Once one pretty well understands the basics of what a shelter is ... what it is supposed to do ... its limitations ... well, then, it is pretty simple to adapt the resources at hand and to make a comfortable camp.

A special thanx to our friend Bill Lansdown of Alva, OK who came and spent nine days with us while we constructed the shelters illustrated here. His strong back and ready wit were a tremendous help.

December 1992

A shelter is simply a barrier between you and whatever is *out there*. Wind, sun, heat, cold, rain, snow, bears ... bears? No bears here. Lets stick to the weather ... the elements.

From the above list what we'll concern ourselves with here is protection from cold and wet. If you can get that under control, making barriers from the other elements (excepting maybe high winds) will be a piece of cake.

We need to keep the water out and we also want to be able to have a fire in or convenient to the house ... preferably inside. We will be using strictly natural materials.

Tho these "ideal" shelters will be constructed with the function of being able to have an inside fire, one must constantly be aware of the very real danger of uncontrolled *fire. Remember always (and I'll be constantly reminding you) that* **we are actually constructing an ideal tinder nest that will be gone in flames in only seconds.** *Real care must be constantly taken with fire in shelters*.

SITE - FLOOR - WALLS - ROOF - SMOKE HOLE - ENTRANCE

These six basics will pretty well cover any of our shelters so let's cover them one at a time.

Site - The location of our house should be the first thing to think about. What do we want it *near* to ... what do we want it *away* from.

Near to trees, bushes, rocks, whatever to help add additional shelter to our shelter ... near to work sites ... near to water (but not in an area that might be prone to flooding if the water level raises) ... near to building materials.

Away from tall trees or other high landmarks which may draw lightning - away from unwanted sounds and sights. Away from any objects that may fall on us - dead tree limbs/rocks from cliffs.

Once you have found the *general* location, look for *specifics* ... high spots. You will want your house to sit higher than the surrounding land in order to shed water. Finding the general location is usually much easier than deciding upon the specific spot to build. Geri and I have spent as much time selecting sites as we have in actual building. Ideally we want a small hillock just the size of our projected house. *This will send whatever rain that falls away from us.* This may seem a simple thing but there have been many occasions that we have witnessed small rivers running thru someone's tipi at some of the rendezvous which we have attended. The water has to go somewhere ... downhill. Digging a trench or building a retainer on the uphill side will sometimes divert water from your bed.

Floor - For all of our shelters, the existing ground will be the floor. It may be padded with leaves, grass, dirt (if on rock) or some other material to your liking. We don't look on the floor, as in modern structures, as something to keep litter free. Dirt comprises most all of our house floors. Softer materials under bedding does make for better sleeping for this aching body tho. Primitives both today and yesterday often poured blood on the floor which then hardened and became rubbery like linoleum. If required, or desirous, to build in a wet area such as a swamp, a network of poles can be laid over a framework to raise you up.

Walls - For protection from the sun alone, walls mite not be needed. For protection from just about anything else walls are a necessity. As we will see shortly, the walls are often integrated into the roof *with the frame*. Sometimes tho, the walls will be separate. In many cases the walls will also support the roof. Sometimes a single thickness wall will do the trick but more often than not for the purposes intended here for protection from water and cold, a double thickness wall will be what we want. Wind and sun ain't all that hard to keep at bay. The interior temperature can be raised considerably with minimal protection. But water has a way of getting through about anything eventually. So, if we can get it waterproof, we got it made.

We'll illustrate here how to incorporate and use rocks in one circumstance. What we find about as simple to construct and most effective, utilizing most materials, is a double row of sticks placed in the ground and filled with litter. This makes for a completely airtight and waterproof wall.

Roof - To us, the roof is one of the most critical segments. It will usually be the most responsible for keeping out the water so here is where we will place what seems to be the most attention. A roof is what makes a shelter.

For our criteria, the roof needs to repel water. Not a real simple task, but also not that difficult if one is aware of some basic rules.

Water runs down. Rule number one. Seems obvious yes but it's surprising how many forget this when building a shelter. Most rains are accompanied by wind which is pushing the water in from the side. Once water hits the roof, it will cease its sideways motion and begin to fall down. What we need to do is slow this fall until it gets beyond the inside of our house.

With a flat roof, once the water hits, it has no where to go but into the house. Flat roofs don't work primitively unless we have a large rock outcropping or something similar. Mostly, just forget about flat.

Now, *the steeper the pitch of the roof, the faster water will run down* it giving it less time to soak thru the materials and come inside.

The *thicker* the covering, the more time it takes the water to get thru.

The *finer* the material used in the covering, the longer it takes for the water to get thru.

Coarser materials call for thicker coverings.

Long grasses make for good coverings. Water will have a natural tendency to follow the stem and leaves of the grasses. Every time that the water hits an obstruction, it will divert from its sideways following of the grass, and fall to the one below it. We need the material to be thick enough so that by the time it works its way around all of the grasses and falls, it will be beyond our living space.

Place the grass upside down on the shelter. As water follows the stem and leaves it will then naturally follow downward . If placed on the way that it grows, whenever it reaches the junction of leaf and stem, it will drip.

Smokehole - Since one major requirement here is the ability to use fire with (and with-in) our house, we will need some method to allow the smoke to leave.

Smoke will naturally seep out of the roof of all these shelters - we just can't get them completely tight with the materials we have at hand, but leaving some other opening, if kept small don't hurt. You'll see four methods in the pages to follow.

Keep the roof space high. Smoke rises. If the interior ceiling is high, on days when the smoke seems to linger, it will be above your heads. In the shelters here illustrated using interior fires, in all cases when we've had fires, we have been able to stand comfortably ... the smoke was well enough ventilated.

Entrance - We of course need some way in and out - and it would also be proper to have some means of closing this off ... a door.

Animal skins have been used forever, raw or tanned. Large pieces of bark ... even grasses rolled into a ball ... a piece of log.

If the lower walls are sealed tight, including the entrance way, you will have less trouble with moving air ... and air moving smoke.

MATERIALS

One thing not to do is to limit your construction to specific materials. Learn to use to the best advantage *any* materials. Integrate. Mix & match.

When constructing a shelter to repel water we want to work mostly with small grass size material which will compress better. Thicker stock such as sunflower stalks, willow or dogwood shoots look

An unbelievably large amount of material is needed in constructing a good shelter. The material shown here made one simple wickiup.

good but require much thicker walls to repel water as there is so much air space for the water to work its way thru.

- Sod
- Dirt
- Wood
- Bark
- Stone
- Grass
- Leaves/litter
- **Lashing material**

It is unbelievable the amount of materials necessary to construct a good weatherproof shelter. The larger size, the more material needed.

If the house is for long term use, make it large enough for however many people - and supplies. The four shelters illustrated here are designed for three to four people. Smaller shelters are easier to heat.

Availability of materials should be real high on the site selection list. It can be real tedious and time consuming hauling materials from any distance at all.

Is there a sequence in building? Well, probably most times. I suppose that it might help to gather materials before you begin any construction ... but then again many times we will just begin with the actual building just utilizing what we come across as far as materials are concerned. Very seldom do we approach building with any actual plan in mind. We just want to end with the best shelter possible under the circumstances. Some might think that for just an overnight shelter that any old thing will do ... but what if you get a goose-drowner rain?

The importance of the roof has been stressed throughout. The foundation and/or framework needs as much attention - it is this that will hold it all together.

Do the best you can with what you have to work with. There ain't much sense in spending a few hours in putting up a roof if it don't repel anything.

A solid tripod is a must as it is the foundation for all that follows. A "Y" in one or more of these three is importand to help lock it if no lashing is available.

The fresh cut cattails had the tendency to slide down so we used bark lashed loosely to help. ———⟶

THE WICKIUP

Warm and comfortable, the wickiup is probably one of the quickest and easiest shelters to construct. Utilizing any number of materials it can be put up in as little as an hour or so if materials are at hand - it can be built to repel most water and a *controlled* fire is possible inside.

The finished product. It stands seven feet inside with a diameter of nine feet (note Geri's head at the door) - will accomodate three comfortably, more in a pinch. This shelter can be made any size. A fire makes it cozy in a hurry ... tho remember to keep it small and attended.

We used three types of materials for covering this
particular house: weeds and cornstalks for one
third, grasses and leaves (litter) for a third and
cattails for a third. These were applied six to eight
inches thick for the most part. Thicker is better.

THE LEAN-TO

The second shelter that we illustrate here is also somewhat of a quickie. This is the shelter that I, John, pretty much grew up with in the Appalachians of Southern New York State 30 to 40 years back.

Now, the basic lean-to that most are familiar with, I find falls far short from qualifying as a real "house" type shelter. By its nature, lean-to's are exposed in one or more directions to the mercy of the wind and any wind driven elements.

When on the trail and using this as a one nighter, this drawback ain't quite as noticeable as it will then be (or should be) built with it's back to the wind, or if fitted with sides, possibly quartering the wind somewhat.

But the wind is a fickle thing ... generally not blowing exactly straight from any one direction but constantly shifting directions some-what. This fact alone makes sides a must (remember that walls needn't shed water so much as wind). If one expects to call this shelter home for any period of time, we find that a coupla variations help considerably to add to your comfort.

You will find in the accompanying illustrations and photo-graphs that we have indeed added substantial walls or sides to the lean-to and also extended these to swing to the front right and left to help block the wind. In addition to this you will be quick to note that we have constructed a wall of sorts to the front of all this by a coupla feet so that the wind is there-by blocked from all directions. This leaves us with approximately a two foot corridor left and right to enter by ... and the fire is placed right in the middle of what little remains of the open area directly in front of the shelter. In actuality what we have done is to construct a chimney for our fire.

We generally build our shelters with the back to the West as that is the direction of the prevailing wind ... in summer we face slightly North of West and in winter we try to face somewhat South of West as the seasonal winds shift accordingly. The day we built this lean-to, the wind was from the North East (preceding a storm) ... the benefit of the East wall was visible with the first fire ... the smoke was blown not into the shelter but up and over it.

The basic framework of lean-to's vary slightly. Here we constructed, though amoungst trees, entirely free standing. There are a multitude of ways of putting it together.

We first need front supports ... these will be supporting the entire structure so use stout materials. On the left we used a simple branched stick and on the right we used two straight sticks to provide the "Y" we are needing. In either case, more strength is obtained by driving the poles into the ground if possible ... or support with rocks if necessary. The sticks on the right are lashed.

Into the "Y" of both we place poles running to the ground (or as you will note in the photos, onto a log to slightly raise the back.

Across these we placed three straight poles as illustrated. From now on we can use crooked poles in the roof and the roof will still remain flat.

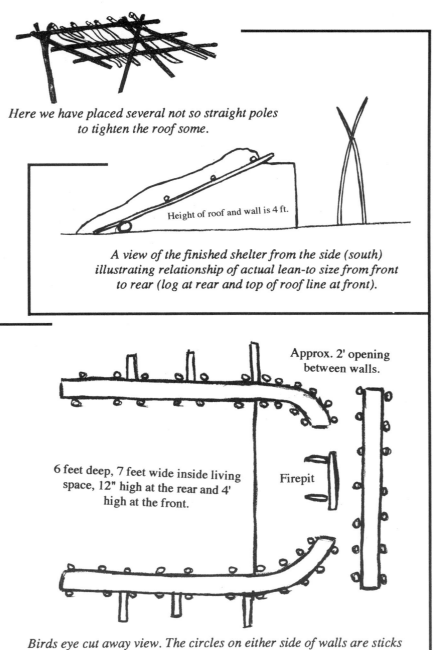

Here we have placed several not so straight poles
to tighten the roof some.

Height of roof and wall is 4 ft.

A view of the finished shelter from the side (south)
illustrating relationship of actual lean-to size from front
to rear (log at rear and top of roof line at front).

Approx. 2' opening
between walls.

6 feet deep, 7 feet wide inside living
space, 12" high at the rear and 4'
high at the front.

Firepit

Birds eye cut away view. The circles on either side of walls are sticks
pushed into the ground, filled in between with sticks/grasses/leaves/weeds
and other litter to provide complete air-tightness ... they support no weight.

Well, now that we've *sketched* it all out for you, lets go to the photos to see if this actually does work.

Initially, some time is spent finding the right site ... most importantly for us here is good drainage. Note the site Geri and Bill are looking over is slightly rounded.

Framing for the roof is complete.

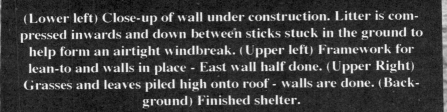

(Lower left) Close-up of wall under construction. Litter is compressed inwards and down between sticks stuck in the ground to help form an airtight windbreak. (Upper left) Framework for lean-to and walls in place - East wall half done. (Upper Right) Grasses and leaves piled high onto roof - walls are done. (Background) Finished shelter.

Thatched Wickiup

With the first wickiup and the lean-to, we've made two of the quickest and easiest shelters to construct that go one or two steps beyond what most think of as "survival" shelters ... tho in many true "survival" situations one would be just as well (or better) off with one of the illustrated "houses" shown here.

But now let us take another step up the ladder in shelter construction. The framework for the wickiup to follow can be put together almost as quickly as the tripod shown earlier but the manner in which we will apply the covering over the most part of the frame is where we will advance.

More, actually *much* more time and effort will be spent in the initial gathering and preparation of materials. Here we will be thatching ... as in tying bundles of grasses into place. This will require the use of more grass as the bundles are compressed as they are tied in place and so tho requiring more time and energy to gather, the resulting house will require less upkeep over time ... the bundles will be as thick as you want (here a good 2") with three layers covering the whole as they are tied overlapping from the bottom up as in shingling.

Some type of lashing material need also be considered. In the example shown on the following pages we utilized basswood bark - simple and easy to find and strip (many other materials are available - reference our book and tape #2 PRIMITIVE FIRE AND CORDAGE).

This style of house in some manner has been used in most areas around the world where the necessary materials exist (not as far as I know in the Arctic) ... in fact it is a common style house in use yet today in some of the remaining primitive cultures.

Tho this may seem somewhat of a difficult project at first, as in many "difficult" projects, the real "difficulty" lies in getting out and doing it. Once the materials were all in one place, the *putting together* took only about six hours time with three of us working.

So, lets do it.

Though we have good photos of the building process, just maybe you'll get a bit better understanding of the all important framework if we line draw some of it also.

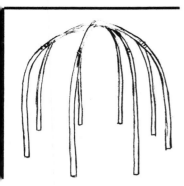

Now, at whatever spacing you desire (we used approx. 18"), lash into place horizontal poles. These not only add stability to the frame but are what we will be lashing our thatching to. The bent door frame we just kinda stuck in - it need not be. We just find that this limits the size of the opening thereby cutting down drafts.

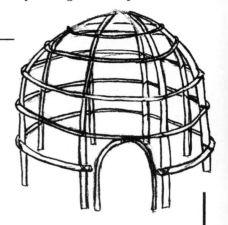

Step one is to gather some green poles somewhat longer than the height of the intended shelter (here we used cedar). Stick the thicker end into the ground (several inches at least) in some semblance of a circle or oval or rectangle (no real rules here ... your choice) ... bend them over and where the opposing tops of pairs meet, lash them securely (they overlap by several feet).

The entire frame can be completely covered with thatch as is, but ... A good way to save on a lot of long thatching grass and to also give yourself a completely airtight lower wall section is to set shorter poles all around the framework about six inches or so out, also placing poles in between the existing uprights (they can be spaced as close as you like ... in fact, the closer together they are, the easier building you will have, being able to use shorter and shorter materials). The in between will be filled with litter You can, in fact, build the entire shelter in this manner, tho the roof wouldn't shed water as well as the longer grasses.

Note the "pointy" top. This ain't necessary but we find that it sheds water better. Nothing more than three cedar limbs lashed together to two cedar "hoops". This utilizes the natural bend of the limb and this all is lashed to the existing frame.

Building the framework.

So lets now take a photo journey while putting together this wickiup to show more clearly some of the steps. The construction of the bottom portion of the wall can be accomplished in several ways utilizing many approaches - we just show one here. The entire structure could possibly be built even better if it all was done in this manner ... which would also make it easier to find materials as you wouldn't be limited strictly to just long grasses ... tho the roof would repel water better if it had a finishing layer of thatching.

Finishing off the lower walls.

The actual job of thatching is not such a project as one might think ... gathering is much more time consuming. One does need consider just what lashing one will use tho. Here we have used basswood bark. You might find it more convenient to splice the lashing as you go so that you end with one continuous cord rather tying off at the end of each length. One wrap around both horizontal pole and the bunch of grass. The bark and grass will shrink somewhat - the grass especially if not dried - and so re-tying may be necessary. The tighter together the bunches are tied, the tighter the finished job. Stagger the thatching so that two thirds are overlapped by the next layer ... this way the entire house will end with three coats. Thatching begins at the bottom (as with shingles) so that moisture runs off the upper layers onto, <u>not into</u>, the lower layer.

The piece we built to point the top - inside and outside view.

Note small size of entranceway in photo at above - easier to close but one must crawl in here. The opening can be made to whatever size you desire.

GENERIC SHELTER

Alright, we've now covered three different basic shelters, two of them quickie, or "survival" types. In the construction of them we've seen three varying frames, roof types and a way to build walls, or sides, simply.

When we build shelters, we usually have only a very basic concept in mind ... certainly no blueprints. Terrain and materials are the two main guidelines.

With this next house we're gonna approach the job at hand with only one concept in mind: I want to use the rock face of one of our revines to form at least one, or better yet two sides of our house.

One benefit of this approach is the fact that, obviously, part of your construction in already done so less time is spent gathering building materials. Another is the fact the you are also placed below ground level so that you are additionally sheltered. In addition, by placing your fire against the rock face, you will store up heat to help warm you thru the night when you don't want a fire burning.

One thing to remember with this trick tho is the fact that many ravines are the result of water run-off ... all of them where water *will* run. We certainly don't want to build in the middle of a possible river when the next rain comes. The secret here is to walk the edges of possible sites and look for places where water don't flow. If the ravines are made due to water running, they still are not excluded. Water won't run over all sides at every spot. - in fact it will usually be a problem only at a few key points. It usually won't be much trouble locating the dry stream beds to avoid ... flattened grass is one sign, worn down to bedrock another. You just don't want to take shelter in your house during a rain only to have it wash you away.

So lets take a walk thru what we did here ...

Site selection was the first consideration. Here Bill and Geri study the prospective site. The pluses: Rocks form two sides for a good height of two and a half feet or so and run-off easy to divert. The minus: The long open side faces North ... nothing we can't overcome.

Bill cleans up the future floor (above) by removing rocks and leveling the earth ... the rocks are temporarily place in position pretty close to where the final walls will end. The birds eye diagram (below) shows what the site was to begin with. Diagrams on the following pages clearly show the progress - especially intermixed with the photos.

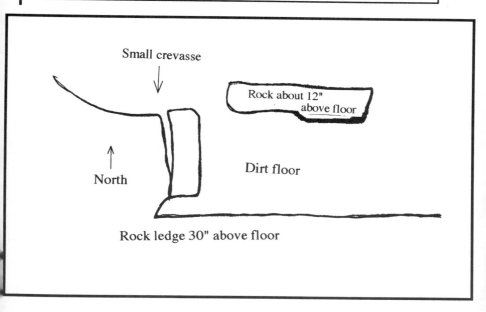

Small crevasse

Rock about 12" above floor

North

Dirt floor

Rock ledge 30" above floor

Rocks were laid to form a wall on the low sides (North and East) about 20" high. Grass was used as a bedding for the rocks so as to create an air tight seal.

On the ledge side most exposed (South), a berm of dirt and rocks was placed to help divert any run-off water ... not so much from the surrounding terrain as from the South side of the roof itself (left).

*(Left & below) A gap betwe
West and South walls serves
as a natural ventilator so we
to build the fire area her
covering the top with flat roc
mortaring them in place usi
clay for the as the mortar.
places a flat rock on chimn
rain cap (right).*

*Note changes in birds-eye drawing
(below) from that of preceding page.
Rock wall laid on North & East sides
... Main support rafter in place
running the length - upright supports
at each end & middle. Ends are braced
from the sides.*

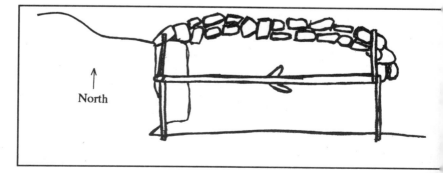

North

For the West wall (or Gable) we elect to use sod since it's close proximity to the chimney will help to prevent possible fire.

Sod wall in place on West (L), Brace pole in place on N & E (top) to hold rafters, Chimney in place and water diversion berm on S. (bottom).

Lashing together the framework. Sod is placed onto the bottom of the S. rafters to add to the water diversion berm (lower right).

405

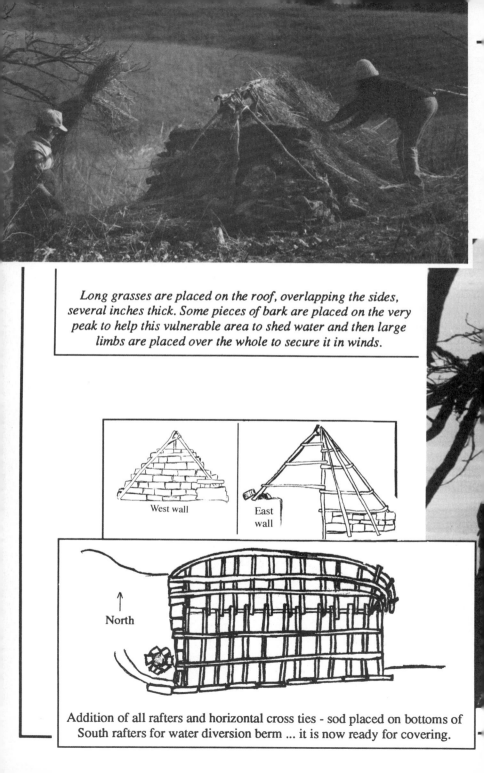

Long grasses are placed on the roof, overlapping the sides, several inches thick. Some pieces of bark are placed on the very peak to help this vulnerable area to shed water and then large limbs are placed over the whole to secure it in winds.

West wall

East wall

North

Addition of all rafters and horizontal cross ties - sod placed on bottoms of South rafters for water diversion berm ... it is now ready for covering.

Time to settle in.

So there you've got it. Four different types of shelters utilizing several methods of construction. Certainly not *one* set of rules or blueprints to follow.

What we hope to have accomplished here is to have shown you how to think a bit for yourself and use some field expedience when it comes to sheltering yourself.

As with most primitive skills, ***there is no one way of doing it***. We teach so that the student is capable of accomplishing the task at hand - successfully. We show characteristics, generically so that you can do these in your own backyard, wherever that may be.

Use what you have and do it your way.